Professor Richard Scolyer ___
Melanoma Institute Austral___
Professor Georgina Long AO. Together, they were named 2024 Australian of Year for their pioneering work in melanoma and for their work in applying that science to brain cancer. Richard is also a senior staff specialist at Royal Prince Alfred Hospital, Sydney, and conjoint professor at the University of Sydney. He is widely regarded as the world's leading melanoma pathologist and one of the world's top melanoma researchers.

In June 2021, Richard was appointed Officer of the Order of Australia (AO) for distinguished service to medicine, particularly in the field of melanoma and skin cancer, and for his service to national and international professional organisations. He has also received multiple awards from many prestigious medical, research and pathology organisations worldwide, and represented Australia as an age-group triathlete.

Garry Maddox is a senior writer at *The Sydney Morning Herald*. A former editor of two film and sports magazines, board member of Sydney Film Festival, playwright and regular host of film and television Q&A sessions, he has been a judge for the Walkley Awards and NSW Premier's Literary Awards, contributed a chapter to the book Baz Luhrmann Interviews, was a finalist for a 2023 International Media Award in Los Angeles and has represented Australia as an age-group triathlete at five world championships.

BRAINSTORM

BRAINSTORM

A dedicated doctor. A devastating diagnosis.
A chance for a medical revolution.

RICHARD SCOLYER

WITH GARRY MADDOX

ALLEN&UNWIN
SYDNEY · MELBOURNE · AUCKLAND · LONDON

First published in 2024

pp. 195–7: Grateful acknowledgement is given to the Nine Network for permission to reproduce quotes from A Current Affair.

pp. 198–9: Grateful acknowledgement is given to Ray Hadley for permission to reproduce quotes from The Ray Hadley Morning Show on 2GB.

pp. 251–4: Grateful acknowledgement is given to Neil Mitchell for permission to reproduce quotes from the Neil Mitchell Asks Why podcast.

pp. 210–2: Grateful acknowledgement is given to the National Press Club of Australia for permission to reproduce quotes from Richard Scolyer's and Georgina Long's speeches.

All photographs are from the family archives unless otherwise credited.

Allen & Unwin
Cammeraygal Country
83 Alexander Street
Crows Nest NSW 2065
Australia
Phone: (61 2) 8425 0100
Email: info@allenandunwin.com
Web: www.allenandunwin.com

Allen & Unwin acknowledges the Traditional Owners of the Country on which we live and work. We pay our respects to all Aboriginal and Torres Strait Islander Elders, past and present.

A catalogue record for this book is available from the National Library of Australia

ISBN 978 1 76147 149 0

Set in 12/18.5 pt Sabon Lt Std by Midland Typesetters, Australia
Printed and bound in Australia by the Opus Group

10 9 8 7 6 5 4 3 2 1

MIX
Paper | Supporting responsible forestry
FSC® C001695
www.fsc.org

The paper in this book is FSC® certified. FSC® promotes environmentally responsible, socially beneficial and economically viable management of the world's forests.

To Katie, Emily, Matthew and Lucy

CONTENTS

CONTENTS

1

DRAMA IN POLAND

It was a Saturday morning. I was in a hotel in a Polish alpine town—an attic room with a stunning view of the snowy Tatra Mountains. I'd felt nauseous when I'd woken in the early hours and was no better by the time my wife Katie, who had been asleep in the bed beside me, was up.

As a doctor, this nausea made me uneasy. I wasn't sure why I felt sick. I was fit and healthy. I hadn't drunk much or eaten anything dubious at dinner the previous night. I knew the important symptoms of heart attacks and strokes, and I didn't seem to have any of them. While I'd always tended to play down being unwell—anxious not to worry anyone—I was worried something was seriously wrong.

I'd planned to call my mum, who lived in a nursing home in Launceston, and figured I'd still do it. After checking the time in Tasmania and ringing her, I had to abruptly end the call when I was overwhelmed with a sudden surge of nausea. I sensed I was about to pass out. I lay on the floor and mumbled something to Katie about how awful I was feeling.

Katie, who is also a doctor, asked me about my symptoms, checked my pulse and felt my forehead. I started to feel cold and shivery, as if I had a fever of some kind. I wasn't sure what was happening. I just wanted to lie on the carpet.

Katie was naturally worried. We talked about my symptoms and ran through the possible medical conditions that might be causing them. There were no obvious signs of a neurological problem, no difficulty speaking or moving my arms or legs and no headache, but it wasn't clear what was wrong.

I wasn't in pain. I asked Katie to get a bin from the bathroom in case I needed to vomit. We wondered if I might have a viral illness, possibly picked up on my travels.

Katie asked if I wanted to move onto the bed to be more comfortable, but I preferred lying on the floor. She gave me a cushion and a rug from the bed but I still felt cold. I covered myself up and said I'd try to sleep.

As I lay there, I was feeling something that I'd never felt before. I had nausea and shivers but what I didn't say anything about at the time was that I also felt strange and fuzzy in my head. I told Katie that she shouldn't worry too much. That I was fine and she should go out and enjoy the day. But Katie decided to stay with me and it seemed to her that I slept for a number of hours. But inside, all I could think was: *I'm going to die, and there's nothing I can do to stop it.* I was panicking. I was scared.

The date was 20 May 2023. We were in Kraków for a conference organised by Artur Zembowicz, a Polish–American professor from Tufts University School of Medicine in Massachusetts. We'd met when I'd organised a symposium at the International Academy of Pathology Congress in Brisbane in 2004. After bonding over a melanoma pathology discovery that we'd been researching independently, we had become good friends.

Both Artur and I were pathologists, diagnosing diseases by examining body tissues mostly with a microscope. As co-medical director of Melanoma Institute Australia and senior staff specialist in anatomical pathology at Royal Prince Alfred Hospital in Sydney, I had spoken at the Kraków conference about melanocytic tumours—pigmented lesions of the skin that are often difficult to diagnose. The all-day talk on Wednesday, presented with Institute fellow Dr Nigel Maher and televised live to medical colleagues around the world, had gone really well.

Fortunately, as it turned out, Katie had joined me in Poland so we could have a few days together after the conference before heading to Ireland, where I was to deliver another talk at the Irish Melanoma Forum in Dublin. The day after my Kraków session, we joined Artur and his wife Margaret, an anaesthetist at Boston Children's Hospital, for a trip to Zakopane, a ski resort close to the Slovakian border.

We had a beautiful day in the snowy Tatra Mountains, catching a horse-drawn wagon to a stunning lake by Rysy, the highest peak in Poland, hiking up past the snowline then walking for two hours back down. Katie and I both enjoyed bushwalking back in Australia, so it had been a great day. The scenery, fresh air and good company were the holiday tonic we needed.

We had dinner with Artur and Margaret at a modern Polish restaurant that evening then caught a taxi back to our hotel. I wasn't feeling myself but didn't mention it to anyone.

The next morning—that terrible Saturday—Katie and I had been due to meet our friends downstairs in the hotel restaurant for breakfast at 9 a.m. I didn't feel anywhere near well enough to go but encouraged her to join them. She was reluctant but headed down to get me something to eat. Artur and Margaret had saved me a piece of Polish cheesecake they said was 'phenomenal', so Katie, who'd been texting to make sure I was okay while she was away, brought it back to the room.

I slept on and off during the morning while Katie read on the bed.

I only remember fragments of what happened over the next three or four hours.

Katie tells me that at about 1 p.m. I stood up, groaned loudly, bent over at the waist and then pitched forwards onto the carpet, grazing the top of my head as it hit the ground. I had a tonic-clonic (grand mal) seizure that probably lasted less than a minute.

Having rushed over, Katie supported me while I lay on the floor unconscious. In the madness of the moment, she couldn't find either of our mobiles or the hotel phone so she opened the door and yelled for help down the corridor. There was no response.

After checking on me again, Katie went back to the door and yelled 'Help!' and 'Ambulance!' in the hope that someone would hear and recognise the English words. Two cleaners came running. As they only spoke Polish, they rang for the hotel manager. After what Katie says felt like ages, the manager arrived, saw what was happening and called an ambulance.

When it arrived, the paramedics, who spoke English, asked Katie all sorts of questions about what had happened. They injected me with a sedative to stop any further seizures and said they'd take me to Zakopane Hospital, the largest of three local hospitals. I remember waking up briefly as they wheeled me on a trolley over rough ground in the hotel car park to the ambulance, and again from a sliding pressure on the trolley as they drove through a roundabout in the town.

When I came around, I was in shock and still panicking. What the hell was happening? Why was I feeling like this?

At the hospital the medical team ran blood tests, an ECG to check on my heart and a CT scan on my brain. I was lucid enough to talk about skin cancer with the efficient young doctor running the emergency unit, who was rushed off his feet.

After the tests, they took me to a critical care area. Katie wasn't allowed in, so she waited outside by herself, unable to get much information from the Polish-speaking nurses and hospital staff.

The results of the blood tests and ECG were normal. While the CT scan appeared to show there had not been a brain haemorrhage, the emergency doctor wanted a second opinion from a radiologist who was not at the hospital— it being Saturday afternoon—so there was a lot of waiting around feeling tired and wondering what had gone so wrong.

Katie had called Artur and Margaret from the hotel as she waited for the ambulance. They had been on a walk high in the mountains but turned around as soon as they heard what had happened. It took them about an hour to get back, and Katie was relieved to see them at the hospital. Both Artur and Margaret, I later realised, took wonderful care of me over the following days. Having trained in Poland before moving to the US, they asked the right questions of the doctor and nurses at the hospital's emergency department and rang colleagues around the country to get me the best possible care, even while none of us knew what was going on.

Around 9 p.m., I was transferred in another ambulance, with Katie sitting beside me, to the bigger Kraków University Hospital 90 minutes away. The paramedics put on the siren whenever there was any traffic around. I remember feeling uncomfortable at one stage, as if I was being tossed around. On arrival, I was admitted to the stroke unit.

I was met by the senior neurology registrar, a hard-working, extremely capable and caring doctor whose name we never caught. In excellent English, she explained to Katie and me what would happen next. I was sent for an MRI scan of my brain and a lumbar puncture, which draws cerebro-spinal fluid from the spinal canal in the lower back.

I arrived back on the ward after midnight and, when Katie, Margaret and Artur left to get back to their hotel, I had an anxious night. I wasn't in pain but I was scared and exhausted. I knew there was a chance the seizure meant I had a brain tumour. That thought filled me with dread and I slept fitfully.

I was still tired when I woke up early the next morning. A hearty breakfast was served to me but I could only manage some buttered bread and a mug of tea.

About 7.30 a.m., the head of the neurology department, Professor Agnieszka Słowik, arrived with a team of junior doctors and nurses. An incredibly impressive, intelligent and caring doctor who also spoke excellent English, the professor had been to medical school with Artur and Margaret. She sat on a chair next to the bed, leaned forward and spoke calmly and reassuringly. She showed me the scan and explained that it showed a 'mass' in my left temporal lobe that was 'most likely a brain tumour'. But there was a small chance the lesion could be a viral infection called herpes encephalitis that was sometimes fatal. In case it was that, she said I needed to start immediate treatment with intravenous antiviral therapy.

I was shocked and found myself falling into a black despair. I realised from the scan and other tests that it was most likely a glioma, a type of brain tumour. I asked lots of questions about whether the lesion could be anything else, what the expected rate of progression was, what the treatment was. She said I needed a biopsy to get a formal diagnosis.

Professor Słowik's advice was to get home as soon as possible for the biopsy and treatment. If it was a fast-growing tumour that caused swelling in the brain, very soon I might not be able to fly at all—on a plane, more swelling could cause seizures. If I needed surgery or if there were complications in Poland, she said I might never make it back to Australia.

When the professor and her team left, it felt like my life as I knew it was over. Working as a neuropathology registrar then staff specialist in pathology at Sydney's Royal Prince Alfred Hospital (RPA) when I was younger, I'd had to diagnose brain cancer many times. I knew the usual outcome for people with a high-grade glioma was shockingly bad.

I felt so many emotions. I was devastated, sad, overwhelmed and despairing. I was terrified it was a fatal diagnosis and anxious about what lay ahead. And when I studied the scan, I was angry that my life was being turned upside down.

———

It had been a busy year at a rewarding time in my life. At the Melanoma Institute back in Sydney, we had continued to make real progress in reducing deaths from melanoma, a cancer that is found at higher rates in Australia than in any other country. We were part of a team of world leaders in pioneering immunotherapy, a relatively new form of treatment that uses powerful drugs to supercharge the body's immune system so it can find and destroy cancer cells. In fifteen years, the five-year survival rate for advanced melanoma had gone from a dismal 5 per cent to a remarkable 55 per cent; tens of thousands of lives around the world were being saved.

We'd made so many advances that, in an outdoors-loving country where once more than 2000 people died from melanoma every year, at the Institute we'd been able to set our sights on zero deaths.

It had been a great time in other ways, too. I loved my life with Katie, who was also a pathologist, and our children: Lucy was fifteen, Matthew seventeen and Emily nineteen. They were all well into their educations, with Lucy in Year 10, Matthew getting ready for the Higher School Certificate, and Emily studying health sciences at the Australian National University in Canberra. They were good kids, too—friendly, outgoing, thoughtful and caring.

We had also finally finished renovations on the house we'd owned in Sydney's inner west for seventeen years, after the disruption of renting a place on the other side of Parramatta Road for a year and a half during construction. We had terrific friends and wonderful relatives. We had been able to go on some unforgettable family holidays. And while I probably worked too hard, I had also been enjoying all the mental and physical benefits of training for triathlons in any spare time I could find.

Less than three weeks before the Polish conference, I represented Australia in an aquathon—a 1-kilometre swim and 5-kilometre run—at the World Triathlon Multisport Championships in Ibiza, Spain. It was a special experience because Emily raced for Australia at the same event.

Between international trips, I'd been travelling with my family to Launceston to see my parents, often catching up there with my brother Mark, who lived with his partner Anna and kids Noah and Maia in Melbourne. We both wanted our kids to have a strong relationship with their grandparents. Despite how hectic it often was, I loved my life.

Now, by myself in a foreign hospital room—with stark cream walls and just a bed, a table and a window overlooking buildings through venetian blinds—I desperately wanted to hug Katie. But there were no tears. I was holding back the overwhelming emotion as I thought through what I'd just been told and what the next steps would be.

While the Polish doctors had been exceptional, none of the nurses spoke English and there was no one to discuss the implications of the diagnosis with. I'd never felt so wildly emotional.

As I've said, it was lucky that Katie was with me on the trip. I had been travelling overseas, mostly by myself, up to a dozen times a year for conferences and meetings. If she hadn't been in that hotel room with me, the seizure might have turned out very differently.

I learned later that Katie was going through the same extremes of emotions as me. Late the previous night in the waiting room, the senior registrar had told her, Artur and Margaret that the MRI scan showed a lesion in my brain. While she would normally tell the patient first, the senior registrar and her boss, Professor Slowik, thought I wasn't well enough to take in the information so they would wait until morning. Katie said her heart had sunk, and she'd felt sick. She instantly understood the implications. She went back to a hotel our friends had booked at the last minute—arriving close to 2 a.m., given that it was some distance away from the hospital—and cried all night.

When Katie arrived in the morning, I burst into tears. All I could say, repeatedly, was 'I'm fucked'. She was crying, too.

Katie left the room to call my executive assistant Kara Taylor and our friend Professor Georgina Long—the Melanoma Institute's other co-medical director—to break the bad news, and to discuss how we could get back home as quickly as possible and start whatever treatment was thought to be best.

I wanted to tell our kids what was happening. So, before Katie had a chance to call them, I FaceTimed Lucy and Matthew, who were being looked after at our place by Katie's sister Sally. I must have looked a worry, wearing a hospital gown and hooked up to an IV drip in a strange room. Lucy asked about the dressing covering the graze on my forehead and I started crying.

I'd always thought it was best to be honest and open and, in my distraught state, I stupidly told them straight out that I had a brain tumour and the outlook was bad. (I don't remember doing this, but was mortified to learn later that this is what I said.) Having thought that their parents were having a brilliant time in Poland, on a rare overseas trip together, they understandably burst into tears, too.

When Katie came back into the room and overheard what I'd done, she called Sally to quickly tell her the bad news so she could comfort the kids. Lucy asked Matthew, then Sally, what a tumour was. Sally called Katie to ask how to explain it to her.

Next I called Emily in Canberra and, when I blurted out the same brutally honest words, we both started crying. Katie called her sister-in-law Sophie, who lived in Canberra, and asked her to head to the uni dorm to be with Emily. When I hung up, Emily FaceTimed Lucy and Matthew to console them and said she'd head to Sydney in the morning.

Breaking bad news is a skill that all doctors need to learn. As my former colleague Professor Chris O'Brien wrote in his book *Never Say Die*, about being diagnosed with a brain tumour, it was best done with 'gentleness, kindness and a sense of hope—that all was not lost and that much could, and would, be done'. In the shock of my diagnosis I'm afraid I lost that perspective, and I apologised later to our kids for how blunt I had been.

Later that morning, Katie called our travel insurer, then the company in charge of what they call 'medical retrieval', about getting back to Sydney. Desperate to distract me as my mind raced across the dire situation, she found some of the family's favourite comedies that she had on her iPad.

As strange as it seemed later, I watched a couple of episodes of *Modern Family* and the movie *The Princess Bride*, which the family reckoned they had watched at least ten times. They were a welcome distraction and unexpectedly comforting.

When Katie eventually had to leave the hospital, the emotional pain and loneliness returned, and I faced another night of restless sleep.

———

That night, I thought through what a brain tumour could do to my mind and body. I knew it could be a glioblastoma, the most aggressive and lethal type of glioma, which was a relatively common brain tumour for men in their fifties like me.

At work, I was used to being in control. I diagnosed more than 2000 melanoma and other cancer cases a year and had delivered talks at more than 400 conferences around the world; I had co-authored more than 900 publications in medical journals and books, and served on the editorial boards of international journals; I had held positions in the World Health Organisation, the American Joint Committee on Cancer and other international bodies; I had mentored younger doctors in melanoma diagnosis, research and treatment, chaired meetings and worked with our team to apply for multimillion-dollar grants to underpin our research. Melanoma Institute Australia, a non-profit organisation largely funded by philanthropy, had an annual budget of more than $20 million and 120 or so very motivated staff.

First thing every Friday morning, we had what was called a multidisciplinary team meeting, which Georgina and I chaired on alternate weeks, to discuss the most difficult cases. It brought together a brilliant group of more than 50 oncologists, surgeons, pathologists, dermatologists, radiologists, radiation oncologists, researchers, nurses, and clinical and support staff, who devised the best treatment plan for each patient. In this confidential environment, the lead specialist's team referred to every patient by their name, age and any factors that were relevant to treatment—medical complications, where they lived, family circumstances—rather than just using a patient number.

Suddenly, instead of diagnosing and helping to manage a patient's life-threatening disease, I had become a patient with a life-threatening disease. I felt like I'd lost control over my life. I'd lost my autonomy.

I was lucky that, at 56, I'd never had a close family member die, but I had known dear colleagues whose lives had been cut short by cancer. One of my closest friends in the RPA pathology department, the talented and dedicated specialist Dr Annabelle Mahar, was just 52 when she died in 2022. I knew Chris O'Brien, a highly skilled head and neck surgeon who became well known through the reality TV series *RPA*. He died from a brain tumour at 57—the age I would be turning later in the year—in 2009.

The next day at the hospital, Katie and I learned how frustratingly difficult it would be to fly home. I was told I couldn't travel for three days after a seizure and needed medical approval to leave Poland, which required another MRI scan with contrast and an electroencephalogram (EEG) test. But even with all those boxes ticked, the retrieval company reps said they were struggling to find a medical escort to administer the antiviral drug through an IV drip, dispense the anti-epileptic medication that was also necessary, and deal with any further seizures or an unexpected medical crisis.

The medical team treating me stressed the urgency of flying back before the likely tumour grew any larger and caused more seizures. But despite calls from Professor Słowik and two of my colleagues in Sydney, Georgina Long and neurosurgeon Associate Professor Brindha Shivalingam, who all gave their approval for me to travel, the retrieval company seemed to be days away at least from flying us home. With growing frustration, Katie and I called them more than a dozen times between Sunday and Tuesday.

Eventually our medical team lost faith in the retrieval company. Professor Słowik and Brindha decided the best plan was for us to get commercial flights home without a supplied medical escort. Instead of an IV drip, they would give me the equivalent dose of antiviral tablets.

On Tuesday at 10.30 a.m., with still no progress on a medical escort, I switched roles from patient to problem-solving doctor. I wanted to take charge and get back some of the control over my life. So I called Qantas and asked how soon we could get flights from London to Sydney. The Qantas rep said there were two seats—one in business, the other in economy—on a flight leaving that night. Once I worked out that we could get to Heathrow in time, I booked them. Then I booked the best available connections: Swiss International Air Lines flights from Kraków to Zürich, then Zürich to London.

I was anxious the airlines might stop us flying if they knew about the brain tumour and the treatment I needed on the flight, so I decided against mentioning it. I knew that international airlines were sometimes very cautious about medical conditions and I was desperate to get home.

While it seemed like we had plenty of time to make all those flights, it was much tighter than expected. I waited for the discharge paperwork to be signed, including a formal summary in Polish and an informal letter in English to show authorities en route if necessary. The wonderful senior neurology registrar on that day, Dr Katarzyna Sawczyńska, was running down a corridor at one stage—with me, keen to get to the airport, jogging alongside her—to organise the paperwork and get my scans on USB sticks in time.

Katie caught a taxi to a distant pharmacy that was the only source of the antiviral drug we could find at short notice. Then she headed to her hotel, packed and checked out. There was no time for her to swing by the hospital, so we took separate taxis and met at the airport.

With our desire to get home overtaking anything else we were feeling, Katie and I had to run to make the flight in Kraków, then again in Zürich. While our luggage went astray and had to be forwarded directly to Sydney, we arrived in London in plenty of time to make the Qantas flight. Under the circumstances, Katie and I agreed that it made sense for me to take the business-class seat upstairs at the front of the plane, with her in the back of economy downstairs.

Relieved to be on the way home, I took sleeping tablets to get some rest from my churning mind. I was eternally grateful for what Katie did on the flight. First, once we were safely on board, she mentioned to the business-class cabin crew that I had a possible brain tumour and she had medication if I had a seizure. They reassured us that they were well trained to deal with all sorts of emergencies, including seizures. We went to our different cabins, confident we were in safe hands.

Then Katie set an alarm to make sure she was awake every four hours to give me the antiviral tablets. While she'd explained the importance of the medication to the staff at the start of the flight, every time the cabin crew rotated she had to go through it again—and get approval—to head from economy upstairs to business. She worked the anti-epileptic tablets into the schedule as time zones changed. It was another example of how fortunate I was that Katie came on the trip.

I'd been blessed with more good fortune, too. It was likely that when we went up Rysy on our trip to Zakopane, the higher altitude had brought on mild brain swelling that caused my seizure the next day. Had we not gone on that walk, I might not have learned about the tumour until it had grown larger and had taken over more of my brain. If I'd been unconscious for an extended period, needed sedation or been unable to make decisions when I was diagnosed, I'd have been be in even worse trouble.

Had Artur and Margaret not been such special friends who understood the Polish medical system, spoke the language, knew Professor Słowik and wanted to find me the best care, I could have been steered to a neurosurgeon who wanted to operate quickly. Instead of flying home, I would have been stranded in Poland.

But these lucky breaks didn't stop me, like many other cancer patients, asking the question: *Why me?* I'd always been fit and healthy. I didn't smoke and barely drank alcohol. I knew the average life expectancy for Australian males was 83—even more if you were a healthy 56-year-old. Depending on the diagnosis being confirmed and the subtype of the tumour, I might not get past 57 or 58.

As flight QF2 landed in Sydney, all I could think was: *What would life be like from now on?*

2

SNAPSHOTS OF A FAMILY

Kicking a football around in Launceston. Walking the famous Overland Track to Cradle Mountain. Long summer holidays camping in the same spot at Ulverstone every year.

My dad did a great job of documenting our family history in Tasmania with decades of photographs. He started in black and white, then bought his first colour camera in 1972. Whenever we were out socialising with family and friends or taking a trip around the state, Dad would get out a small Olympus or Canon, which he carried around in his pocket, and start clicking away.

His dedication to recording our lives fills 80 albums, each with 100 photos, that are filed by number and date on shelves in his living room. These 8000 photos are a treasure trove that shows Dad's love for our family. I always enjoy going through them when I go back to Tassie on holidays. While I've never been anywhere near as meticulous at taking and filing photos, I've surrounded myself with pics of Katie and our kids in my office. Up on a shelf, the kids are eating ice creams or smiling in front of a tree at a long-forgotten get-together in a park. They're having fun in a swimming pool, enjoying an overseas holiday or getting ready for school in their new uniforms. Even before I was diagnosed with a brain tumour, family pictures that came up on my iPhone from years ago could bring tears to my eyes.

Take out just about any album from the early years on Dad's shelves and it will show what an active kid I was. With blond hair and a cheeky grin, I hammed it up for the camera as I played sport, camped, swam, went walking in the bush, rode my bike and explored.

I enjoyed the attention then. I'm quieter as an adult. Now I'm driven by wanting to help other people rather than getting pats on the back. But, deep down, when I'm presenting at a conference or making a speech to highlight skin cancer awareness, I still don't mind the attention.

Born on 16 December 1966, at Queen Victoria Maternity Hospital in Launceston, northern Tasmania, I was underweight as a baby, scrawny as an infant and often sick with tonsillitis. While some health issues my mum suffered made things hard in my early years, I thrived after I had my tonsils out at the age of five and started primary school. The kind teachers, my family, my friends, playing sport— I loved it all. What I learned as a kid in Tassie, especially the values I admired in my parents, set me up for life.

Our parents, Jenny and Maurice, brought up my older brother Mark and me in a red-brick house at 1 Fairway Crescent, Riverside, a suburb of Launceston bordered by the Tamar River and bushland. As the street name suggests, we were near the Riverside golf course.

Playing as kids, we would always be able to smell the fresh, often damp bushland and regularly saw kangaroos, wallabies, possums—and sometimes even Tasmanian devils scurrying away quickly. There were birds everywhere, including kooka- burras and sparrows, and plovers that swooped at intruders during the breeding season. I always hoped there was some truth to supposed sightings of the extinct Tasmanian tiger around the state but, unfortunately, there never was.

Mum was a primary school teacher and Dad was an auto electrician. Dad's job only allowed him two weeks' holiday a year, so during my years at Riverside Primary School, he retrained and switched to TAFE teaching, which meant he could spend more time with Mark and me.

Our parents were both very caring, and we felt like we were the most important things in their lives. I knew Mum loved and wanted the best for me. One small example: as a kid, I had some kind of allergy that meant wool made me very itchy, so she stitched cotton skivvy sleeves inside all my woollen jumpers.

Dad was gentle and practical. He loved sport, especially Australian Rules, which he'd starred at when he was younger. He encouraged Mark and me to get involved in team sports, so I played Aussie Rules, cricket and basketball. After racing the odd triathlon, I took it up more seriously in my forties. While it seems like a solo sport, competing in triathlons brought me into a community of enthusiastic people that often feels like a team. I've never stopped enjoying all the physical and mental benefits of exercise and sport.

Even though we were always playing games or going off to swim together, Mark and I weren't especially close as kids. He was two years older and much taller than me, but I was pretty domineering. I liked to decide what games we were going to play and who was on whose team.

I could be mean and would sulk if I didn't win. I didn't like that Mark would tease me about things—such as how I kicked a football. When I was little, I used to drop it with two hands, rather than one, so I could guide it down. That teasing made me want to do it right, so I practised until I could do it one-handed. I always found it frustrating not being as big or as good at sport as him, so I tried harder. I've never lost that gritty determination to succeed at whatever I'm doing.

Mark won my absolute admiration in primary school when what I now know was a herpes virus affected his eyesight. These days, a patient would be given acyclovir drops to clear it up, but the treatment was very different in the early 1970s. Mark was held down while the GP used a scalpel, without any anaesthetic, to scrape the surface of his right eye. Dad had to leave the room because Mark was crying out so loudly in pain. I wasn't there but when I heard about it, I felt sick. I couldn't believe how brave he was.

It wasn't until years later that I realised how kind—and protective—Mark had been to me growing up. He would go easy on me when we were wrestling or playing a game. He has become a very caring husband and father. Now, with families of our own, we are much closer than we once were.

———————

A family tree on the wall of our house in Launceston went back to the 1600s. My cousin Greg, who did the research, traced the Scolyers back to Cornwall, in south-west England, where they had the surname 'Collier'—which may have meant they were coalminers. That morphed into 'Scolyer', possibly when an initial 'S' in a Christian name was added to the surname.

The Scolyers arrived here by ship in the 1850s, just after the penal colony of Van Diemen's Land was renamed Tasmania. Greg said there were three generations in the state before Dad was born—the second youngest of ten children—in 1935. He grew up on the family farm at Bridgenorth, north-west of Launceston.

Dad was ten when his father, Mervyn, died of a heart attack. He was only 54 but had struggled for decades with the effects of gassing and shrapnel wounds in France during World War I. After his death, Mervyn's widow, Linda, moved the family to a new house in nearby Riverside. They had turned into an extended family for me of aunts, uncles and cousins. When we were kids, many of them lived within 5 kilometres of our place and we socialised together regularly.

Dad, his brothers and his cousins were keen Aussie Rules footballers. The Scolyer boys are said to have made up nearly half the Bridgenorth Parrots team in the Tamar competition in the 1940s and '50s. I kept up the family connection when I trained with the mighty Parrots during university holidays one winter. Decades later I was invited to become their number one ticketholder.

My parents met at a dance when they were both eighteen. Mum was at the University of Tasmania studying arts; Dad had left school at fourteen and was an apprentice mechanic at the time. He said there was 'electricity' when they met.

Dad was a talented enough Aussie Rules player to be recruited by the St Kilda club in Melbourne, which was part of the Victorian Football League (VFL), now known as the Australian Football League (AFL). But Mum didn't want to live in Melbourne, and football wasn't the lucrative career that it would later become, so they stayed in Tassie.

I've often wondered why he didn't insist. What a landmark in his life it could have been! But Dad doesn't have any regrets about the decision. He loved Mum deeply and didn't want to leave her. Even in his late eighties, he's still so passionate about AFL that he'll sometimes travel interstate to watch a match.

One of my uncles, Roy Apted, who married Dad's sister Valerie, did go to Melbourne to join St Kilda. He played 44 games as a backman from 1959 to 1963. Roy and Valerie's daughter Maree, who is three days younger than me and lived three streets away, was one of my closest friends throughout my childhood.

Like the rest of my family, I was a huge St Kilda fan until the 1971 grand final, when they played Hawthorn. It's a running joke in the family that I changed teams at half-time. I decided that I absolutely loved Peter Hudson, Hawthorn's champion full-forward who was from Tassie, and was impressed by how committed and skilful the team was. I was the only member of the family who was happy when Hawthorn won by seven points. Perhaps I knew my own mind early, and wasn't troubled about upsetting anyone. I know it wasn't because they were going to win: Hawthorn were two points down at half-time.

Take out another album and there's a photo of me in the Hawthorn jersey that my parents bought after forgiving me for changing teams. I wore it almost every day in winter. I came to love two other Hawks players: star rover Leigh Matthews and centre half-back Peter Knights, who had blond hair like me and took spectacular marks.

As an adult, I like to weigh up situations and make strategic decisions, even when it comes to football. So, now that I live in Sydney, I've changed teams again to the Sydney Swans. This means that Katie, our kids and I can go to games together and all cheer for the same team.

As well as photos of us kids, Dad's albums include photos of my parents getting married in 1958. They look so young and excited about life. Six years later, Mark was born and I came along two years after that. The delay meant Mum was 30 and Dad was 31 when they became parents, which was old for the time. When I asked them about this as a teenager, they were honest and told me about the challenges they'd had with fertility. That was the kind of thoughtful and considerate parents they were, and still are.

Mum had a tough early life, though. As the oldest of six kids—two girls and four boys—she had to carry far more of the household load than most children do. Her dad was a stern primary school principal whose transfers around Tassie meant the family had to keep moving house. While living on the west coast, where it rained for something like 275 days a year, she remembers being almost a substitute mother to her young brothers, always trying to dry nappies in front of a fire.

After proving she was smart in high school, Mum was having a fine time at uni when her father told her she had to drop out and go to teachers' college, presumably because he thought she should get a job. She felt like her wings had been clipped. It seems sexist to me and, not surprisingly, she resented it. With such a strict father, she would have appreciated how kind and generous my dad was when they met.

While Mum switched to teaching, her four younger brothers were all allowed to go to uni. Two of them, Phil and Tony, became medical doctors; Adrian was an engineer,

Rod studied science, and they both went on to get PhDs. Mum's only sister, Rose, went overseas, met her future husband Alan on a Contiki tour around Europe and went to live with him in Johannesburg.

Missing from the photo albums are the more difficult times in our family history.

My earliest memory—I was three—is Mum having what we later learned was a stroke right as 1969 turned into 1970. When she collapsed at a party on New Year's Eve, other partygoers thought that she'd drunk too much. Mum had two more strokes in January, leaving her with a weak right side and trouble speaking. Doctors eventually put the strokes down to her being on the oral contraceptive pill, which, at the time, was high in oestrogen and was associated with an increased risk of blood clots forming.

Mum and Dad went to Melbourne for a week of rehabilitation. When they came home, Mum was hardly able to get out of bed, and struggled to walk and talk. She had a squash ball by her bed that she'd use to strengthen her right hand. I'd sit with her to keep her company, and sometimes play with the ball.

Then came an even more worrying incident. As Dad describes it, Mum was finding her life really difficult, with the effects of the strokes and the demands that lay ahead. So she tried to end it by taking too many tablets. Thankfully, she was found before major damage was done. I can imagine how desperate she must have felt to have her life upended by ill health in her thirties.

Mark and I share a memory from when we were young kids that we're not sure relates to one of Mum's strokes or her overdose. We were at home when she fell to the floor. We were upset when she couldn't get up or speak properly. Mark called a neighbour, who rang an ambulance. We heard its siren from the yard—our neighbours had sent us outside to play—and they took her to hospital.

After she tried to end her life, Mum had to go to Melbourne then Hobart to recover. Years later, we learned that she went to a psychiatric hospital for six months. Dad went with her—staying as long as his work allowed—while family and friends looked after Mark and me.

Dad arranged for Mark, who had started at Riverside Primary, to stay with our Aunty Bev and Uncle Max; their kids, our cousins Michael and John, were also at school. But because she taught at the school, my aunt couldn't look after a preschooler, too. So I was sent to be cared for by another aunt and uncle, Lily and Roy Horton, an older couple who lived on a remote farm at Winkleigh, 40 or so kilometres away, for more than six months.

I loved them both, but while my aunt was gentle and caring, my uncle was a tough farmer. Sometimes he was kind and let me ride on his tractor; other times he seemed angry and I was scared. I cried under the table when they fought, worried about what might happen.

It was only decades later that I recognised how I react as an adult might be influenced by this time on the farm. I think it taught me to close off and be more self-reliant.

It might also have made me sometimes run away from problems, hiding my emotions rather than facing up to them directly. Mark thinks both of us learned to be more independent when we were separated from our parents and that, because I was younger, it had more of an effect on me.

When we were all back living in Riverside, Mum was more fragile and emotional than she had been before the strokes. When she cried or got angry, Mark and I would try to cheer her up. As sad as I was about what she was going through, I felt helpless to make her better. But Mum showed real determination to overcome her health crises. I admire how my parents got through these life-altering events together.

Before the strokes, Mum had been teaching Kindergarten to Year 2 at Riverside Primary. Afterwards she couldn't get a teaching job in the public education system, so Dad spoke to the nun in charge of St Anthony's, a Catholic primary school in Riverside. She said Mum could do some voluntary work there.

That turned into a part-time job as a teacher's aide; then, when Mum had almost fully recovered from everything she'd faced, she became a full-time teacher again. Religion was never part of our upbringing but I appreciate, as an adult, it was a Catholic school that helped get Mum back to work.

Mum's health problems eventually gave me a strong desire to help people as a doctor. I thought it was important to do whatever you could to make life better for the people you loved when they were struggling.

———

Dad's albums also include photos of Mark and me in our school uniforms. At Riverside Primary, I found schoolwork easy and really enjoyed maths. But I never did any study until I had to, and I was slow learning to read. I much preferred to kick a footy than pick up a book.

In Year 2, my teacher was Mrs Scolyer: my Aunty Bev. When we were asked to read a book independently for class, I wanted to keep up with my friend Cam Matthews, who was a quicker reader than me, so I skipped some pages. A school supervisor then tested us, and when it became obvious that I hadn't read the whole book, she made me go back to the start and point to every word as I read it aloud. It was embarrassing—an early blow to my ego.

By then, I was already competitive. I wanted to be the best at everything, and I didn't try to hide it, as I learned to do when I became an adult. I realised my reading had to improve, and it did, via my interest in magazines and comics rather than books. I loved magazines about VFL and cricket. Stylish batsman Greg Chappell was my cricket idol, tearaway quick Jeff Thomson was my favourite bowler, and I knew all their stats from the magazines I read. Even now, as an adult, I never read books for enjoyment—just for study or work.

Try another album and there's a photo of me, aged nine, building a raft out of milk cartons at home. I'd seen how to do it in a magazine that my Uncle Ady, who lived in Canada, had sent me one Christmas. I thought it would be an adventure and, like Dad, I liked building things. As a kid, if I wanted to do something, I did it. It was an early sign of the ambition, determination and possibly stubbornness that I have as an adult.

I collected milk cartons, and when I had enough I built my raft. It had a wooden frame, with chicken wire covering the cartons and a sheet of plywood on top. Dad helped with sawing and buying the plywood. Mark also assisted, but I wanted to be in charge.

When the raft was finished, Dad loaded it into his station wagon and the family headed to the dam at the Frosts' place up Muddy Creek Hill in Legana, a short drive away. I was rapt when it floated. I stood on it and paddled out, proud of what I'd built. Making the raft taught me to aim high and apply myself. I remember one of my high school teachers saying, 'Aim for the sky and you'll get to the treetops. Aim for the treetops and you won't get off the ground.' I took it to mean: 'Be ambitious and you'll achieve more.' This is something I've taken with me as I've tried to make a difference in medicine, and it's something I've tried to instil in my kids.

As children we would build forts; one year, my friend Cam, some other kids and I tunnelled through thorny berry bushes to build a fort out of plywood that we'd found in the marshy ground near the river. We blocked up the entrance with bushes when we left to keep out intruders.

Another year, when I went exploring with my friend Tim Sutton and his sisters, Catherine and Alison, we built a fort out of hay bales in a farmer's shed. They were so heavy that it took a couple of us to move each one. Sometimes a bale would fall down but, happily, none landed on us. While we saw snakes there—and they're all deadly in Tassie—we managed to avoid being bitten. When I was in Year 9, Dad helped me with a more ambitious project: building a model of an internal combustion engine, which was fun.

Even though our parents gave us pocket money for tidying our rooms and other household tasks, they encouraged Mark and me to get part-time jobs, so we took on a paper run together. On Saturday evenings, we'd wait at the Riverside supermarket until a guy drove in with the Saturday night edition of *The Examiner*, which was popular because it included the VFL results. We'd fill up our wooden cart and take the papers around the streets, knocking on doors until 8.30 p.m. If we were lucky, someone who'd had a drink or two would give us a massive tip.

On other nights, we watched TV. Our parents loved *Bellbird*, an ABC show about the residents of a small country town. I preferred police shows like *Starsky & Hutch* and *The Streets of San Francisco*, and Paul Hogan's comedy show. Hoges was my idol as a kid. I wanted to be like him, although Dad's early home movies suggest I was more like his dimwitted offsider Strop! Like many Australians of our generation, Mark and I were obsessed with the music show *Countdown*. I liked the Australian bands who were on it:

Skyhooks, Sherbet, Ted Mulry Gang, Hush, Dragon and AC/DC.

When colour TV reached Australia in 1975, Dad was proud to get one. After he put it on a stand, Mark and I were rolling it to a different room when the TV tilted forward and fell over. We thought we'd been lucky because the screen didn't smash. But when the picture started to deteriorate we had to own up. Conveniently, I have no memory—in either black and white, or colour—of how we were punished.

———

Throughout my childhood, our extended family in Riverside was the focus of many social activities.

My cousin Maree and I had a big group of friends in common, and we all hung out together outside school hours. She was smart, popular at school and better at sport than me, shining at netball, softball, volleyball and athletics. Maree helped me to recognise the importance of being open and honest. She now says I was 'conservatively rebellious' as a kid: I'd muck around and play jokes on people but never did anything that would upset my parents. While she thinks my mother's health problems affected me as a boy, she always thought I seemed optimistic and positive.

Some photos in Dad's albums show the males in the extended family—all the uncles and cousins—getting together for social occasions. Every Wednesday night, we'd meet at a different house to play eight ball (pool), snooker or indoor bowls. We'd all watch the VFL grand final together every year. While Maree came along sometimes, it seemed normal at the time that it was mostly men and boys getting together. While it was a supportive community, I can see now that excluding women and girls so often wasn't right.

On weekends, the extended family held parties for often 40 people, and 'bring a plate' was the rule. We had such a close group of relatives that if one family decided to renovate their house, everyone would go over on the weekend to help out. When another family decided to renovate, we'd all head to their place next.

Over summer, we'd play cricket with my cousins, uncles and friends, with our games starting after dinner and going until 9 p.m. or even later. Dad wasn't competitive; he just enjoyed playing. Mum preferred to stay inside reading novels and watching TV, but was happy for us to play outside as long as we wanted.

If you loved sport the way I did, Launceston was an outstanding place to grow up. It's a small city with an outdoor lifestyle that's famous for producing champions. In recent decades, they have included swimmer Ariarne Titmus; cricketers David Boon, Ricky Ponting and George Bailey; cyclist Richie Porte; triathlete Jake Birtwhistle; racing driver Marcos Ambrose; boxer Daniel Geale; and distance runner Stewart McSweyn. A lot of star Aussie Rules players came from Launceston, too, including Brent Crosswell, Craig Davis and David Grant, who was a good friend of mine in high school.

Mark and I weren't champions but we were always kicking the footy in the backyard or playing cricket. Snicking the ball above a line on the garage door meant you were out; so did hitting a tree on the full, knocking it into the next-door neighbour's yard—that was six and out—or hitting a passing car on the road. Our backyard footy games expanded over the years until we were playing on the gravel and asphalt car parks of the Presbyterian church hall or swimming pool across the road.

This sporty childhood included Cam's parents taking us to Little Athletics. While he was good at everything, I enjoyed running best, and did well in the 800-metre and 1500-metre races. Sometimes I won. As I grew taller than other kids my age, I became stronger at the 60-metre hurdles and long jump, too.

While there must have been only 50,000 people in Launceston, it was the home of four of the six Aussie Rules teams in the Northern Tasmanian Football League: Launceston, North Launceston, East Launceston and City-South. Dad often took us to watch the Blues—Launceston, the team he'd played for—at Windsor Park on Saturday afternoons. The way the ground was designed, rainwater pooled in the middle rather than running off at the sides, so it was always muddy. My favourite player was a portly full-forward with a beard, Bob Smith, who was a master at milking free kicks. As soon as he'd win one, he'd jump up and show the crowd that he'd faked it.

I played for the Blues from under 11s but while dreaming, like many kids do, of playing VFL, I knew I was never going to be good enough.

Another of Dad's albums has photos of Mark and me as swimmers. For three or four years, we swam with a squad run by Margaret Malone, who was a state-level swimmer, and often her dad, too. We'd get up early six days a week, while our parents were still in bed, and cross the road to the Riverside Aquatic Centre, a 33-metre outdoor pool that was only open in the warmer months. After school, we'd train or race every weeknight and again on Saturday mornings—thirteen sessions a week.

While I was always competitive, I was never as good as the best swimmers in the squad. Mark and I really enjoyed it and made some good friends, but we eventually realised there was more to summer than all that training, especially if we weren't going to be the best in the state. Mark came closest when he won a silver medal in the 50-metre backstroke at the Tassie championships one year.

There were always other sports to try.

During the Australian Open or Wimbledon, we'd play tennis on an asphalt court at Riverside High until it was dark; Björn Borg was my favourite player. We'd play golf at the Riverside course. One time a friend's dad gave him boxing gloves so we could fight each other, but when someone got hurt and lost his temper, I remember thinking, 'This is stupid!' and we stopped.

There are treasured photos in one album of a sporting highlight of my childhood. One summer, while we were on holiday in Ulverstone, Dad, Mark and I—aged ten— caught the train from our campsite to the New Year sports carnival at Burnie on the north coast. We saw one of the most legendary events in Tassie sporting history when Danny Clark, a future five-time world cycling champion, won the Burnie Wheel Race by chasing down the leaders from the back mark in a handicap race.

Watch the video on YouTube and there's a deservedly famous commentary by an old footballer and cyclist called Harold 'Tiger' Dowling. 'One lap to go, it is, in the final of the Burnie Wheel Race, and here's a go if ever you've seen one,' Tiger says, getting more and more excited as Clark goes out after the leaders who are a long, long way ahead.

'You wouldn't believe it! Danny Clark has won the Burnie Wheel Race! It's just *unbelievable*. He was 150 metres behind them with one lap to go . . . I've never ever in my whole born days seen anything like that. I'm completely speechless!'

Mark and I—and the rest of the crowd—went crazy. The local paper, *The Advocate*, called Clark's ride 'the eighth wonder of the modern world'.

I'm grateful to Launceston for giving me a love of sport. Whenever my work life has been stressful, exercise has been tremendous for my mental and physical health. When I was diagnosed with brain cancer, it helped ease my anxiety. I'd set out for a run or a cycle at dawn, arriving home with a sense of wellbeing that lasted throughout the day. It lifted my spirits. I've been so pleased that Emily, Matt and Lucy have also enjoyed playing sport.

But sometimes my own love of it as a kid brought pain. In Year 6, when I was eleven, my friends and I would play cricket with a composite ball (made of plastic-coated cork) on a concrete pitch before school and at lunchtime. Some of the guys bowled fast, and—madness!—we didn't wear pads or helmets. More of a batter than bowler (though not really good at either), I tried to hook a full toss; the ball hit my finger and broke it. A teacher told me to run it under cold water. When that didn't work, I had an X-ray—then got a cast and, later, a splint. That set my sporting career back for a while.

———————

What you don't often wonder about as a child is what your parents were like when they were younger. In the 1960s and early '70s, Mum and Dad were so passionate about the Tassie wilderness that they flew into Lake Pedder to join the protests to stop it being flooded for a hydroelectric scheme. The conservationists lost when the lake was flooded in 1972, but the environmental movement grew to the point where protesters from around the country later stopped the planned flooding of the Franklin River.

My parents instilled this love for the Tassie environment in us. On weekends and in school holidays, they took us on adventures to all the state's national parks, and even to less scenic places like the mining town of Queenstown on the west coast. When Mark and I were young they also signed us up for Cubs—junior Scouts—where we learned not only practical outdoor skills but lessons in leadership and the importance of contributing to the community.

Grab an early photo album from Dad's shelf and you'll find a picture of me, aged six, on one of my first overnight camping trips at Wineglass Bay on Tasmania's east coast. With a group of friends, Dad, Mark and I went for a bushwalk, with everyone carrying a backpack, then camped overnight and walked out. It felt special to be surrounded by so much natural beauty in the bush by the sea.

Photos from different years show our summer holidays at Ulverstone, 120 kilometres from Launceston, on the state's north coast. Our family booked the same spot at the same campsite every year to pitch our tent—it was white with a green roof and a pole down the middle. We headed there around Christmas and usually stayed until just before school went back in February. When I was eight, we upgraded to a caravan while keeping the same camping spot. Once we arrived to set up camp and found someone else in our spot; Dad got upset, so they had to move.

A family called the Castles, who were also from Launceston, always had the campsite next to us. Our relatives and other families from around Tassie stayed in their usual spots every year as well. Friendships were rekindled very quickly each year, especially for the kids.

Every day at Ulverstone we'd go down to the beach and—embarrassingly, given my later work in melanoma prevention—we would often apply baby oil to speed along our tans. If it wasn't raining, we'd swim up to ten times a day. If it *was* raining, we'd put on our crappy raincoats and still go out to play.

With Maree, Maree's brother Malcolm and other holidaying kids, we'd play cricket, either on the beach or on an old golf course behind the campsite, and hide-and-seek and chasings in the dense boobialla trees near the beach. We'd buy fish and chips from the shop near the camping area and walk along the railway tracks into town to buy comics. Sometimes the parents would play golf or tennis.

These were the sort of relaxed holidays—bonding experiences full of lasting memories—that I wanted for my family when Katie and I had kids. When we've visited my parents in Launceston, I've taken them to some of the places I loved growing up. Tassie, especially its stunning wilderness, feels like it's part of my DNA.

Slide out another album and you'll see one more highlight of my adventurous childhood: family trips to Cradle Mountain in the remote Tasmanian wilderness. We'd go a couple of times a year, with the Frosts, the Suttons and some other families, to do a walk. Even if there was snow on the ground, we still walked.

While I was in infants school, we did a full-day walk with some friends and their families up the lower slopes of Cradle Mountain and around Dove Lake. It would have only been 10 kilometres, but the terrain made it tough. Afterwards we were so cold and wet in our raincoats that our parents put us in the back of the station wagon with the heater on—outer clothes off, huddling together, shivering under blankets—to warm up.

I was ten when I walked the famous Overland Track for the first time. It's a 65-kilometre track from Lake St Clair to Cradle Mountain. We did it in five days, carrying our tents, water, food and everything else we needed in our metal-framed backpacks. Dad organised the trip, and our group included Mark, our cousin John and two of our uncles, Phil and Rod.

Dad trained Mark and me on our holiday in Ulverstone before the hike to make sure we were ready. He'd get us to run all the way to the end of the beach and back—maybe 5 kilometres—every day, and send us off for walks carrying backpacks loaded up with an iron or a heater.

The biggest challenge on the Overland Track came as we approached Cradle Mountain on day five: the weather started to turn bad, which can be incredibly dangerous in the Tassie mountains. In 1965, the year before I was born, a group of teachers and students from Launceston's Riverside High had set out on a five-day walk from Lake St Clair and were caught in near-blizzard conditions around Dove Lake, near the end of the walk. Tragically, fourteen-year-old David Kilvert and teacher Ewen Scott died. But that school group was walking the track in late May; we were walking in January.

As our nominated walk leader, Dad made the sensible call to change routes so we wouldn't be so exposed if it snowed. As it turned out, it didn't snow and we made it all the way. It was a magic walk: climbing up mountains with views of pristine wilderness, swimming in a river that was so cold it took your breath away, setting up camp in a clearing (we stayed outdoors for two nights and in huts for the other two), cooking pasta and noodles on a methylated-spirits stove, sitting around a campfire talking and singing, and looking up at the incredible view of the stars. When we went home to Launceston, I was so fit after the training at Ulverstone and the walk at Cradle Mountain that I broke a local 1500-metre running record for under-eleven boys.

Another album from the shelf has photos of my first trip to Sydney, when I was eight, on a family holiday. After we caught a ferry across Sydney Harbour to Taronga Zoo, Mark and I split up from Mum and Dad to see different animals. Then the two of us became separated—I reckon Mark ran away from me—and suddenly I was lost in an unfamiliar place in a new city.

I didn't know what to do. I headed back down to the ferry terminal, thinking everyone would have to leave that way eventually. I was sitting there, crying, when an adult came up to help. Mum and Dad half-heard an announcement about a lost boy on the PA. 'I think that was Scolyer,' Dad said. They rushed to the top entrance of the zoo, then learned they had to head back down to the bottom. It was a huge relief when I saw them.

———

Throughout my childhood, Dad's dedication to family photographs was almost obsessive. He always bought two sets of prints when the film was processed—one set that everyone could hand around and get their fingerprints on, the other that he would keep in perfect condition for the album. His collection of albums is cherished by our family.

Just before I started high school, Dad took his camera—and his new long and wide-angle lenses—on an overseas family holiday that opened my eyes to a different world.

3

FINDING A FOCUS

I had just turned twelve when my parents took Mark and me to South Africa. I didn't realise it then, but it was a volatile time there: Nelson Mandela was still in prison, apartheid was still in place and there'd been protests, murders and bombings.

My parents, who had always been socially progressive, were very aware of apartheid and the political tensions. But the trip was about visiting Mum's sister Rose and her South African husband Alan. Rose had two sons, Chris and Andy, who we were excited to see again.

It was my first overseas trip. The extended Scolyer family held a party for us in Launceston and seemed to be thinking, 'We're never going to see you again.' No one on Dad's side of the family had gone overseas before, let alone somewhere that had been on the TV news because of the Soweto uprising a couple of years earlier.

I was awestruck at how massive the plane was that flew us from Melbourne to Johannesburg. It felt like a long way— it *was*—and I slept on the floor. Before I fell asleep, though, there was so much that was fascinating: how many people there were on the plane, the way we were served food, the fact that everyone watched a movie on a screen at the front of the plane at the same time, and how there was a non-smoking section next to a smoking section. Looking back on it as an adult, it seems crazy that passengers could smoke on planes.

I enjoyed meeting Rose and her family.

After Christmas, eight of us packed into a small station wagon to drive to Kruger National Park, with a trailer on the back carrying our luggage. As soon as we arrived, my uncle pointed out a giraffe, then backed up so everyone could get a better view. But he'd forgotten about the trailer—we heard a crash as it jack-knifed.

Dad started to jump out of the car to see what had happened, until everyone screamed for him to get back in. He'd forgotten that everyone had to stay in their cars in the game reserve because of all the wild animals. It was a sweltering hot day, and the station wagon didn't have air conditioning, but it was amazing to see elephants, lions, leopards, impalas, hyenas and kudu up close. I'd seen so many kangaroos, wallabies, possums and snakes in Launceston, but seeing these South African animals in their natural habitat after only knowing them from TV and schoolbooks was spectacular. We had four more days touring around the national park and I enjoyed every minute of them.

We stayed in South Africa until the end of January, visiting Pretoria, Durban and Cape Town, with Dad taking lots of photos. I had my arm in a sling for a while after falling out of a tree I'd climbed in the rain.

My parents took us to Soweto—they wanted to see what it was like in the township and to understand what had happened. I think we were one of the first international tour parties allowed in after the rioting and it was eye-opening. As we toured around, the kids in the streets were incredibly friendly, laughing as they touched my blond hair, as if it was something they'd never seen before. Many were living in desperately poor conditions, in tin huts, but they seemed to find so much joy in life. It felt like I was being mobbed by new friends.

On the way home, there was a scary experience when our plane circled for an hour before landing to refuel in Mauritius. When I saw fear in the faces of the flight attendants, I became anxious—it didn't look good. 'Oh well, we've had a great holiday,' Mum said, lightening the mood. 'I don't mind if it ends now.' Fire engines lined the runway as we approached, but we landed safely. The captain announced that it had been a false alarm caused by a faulty landing gear light.

Arriving back in Launceston, I felt lucky to live in Australia, but the trip had opened my eyes to how extraordinary the world was. It sparked a desire to travel more and learn about different cultures.

Years later, I admired my parents for wanting to see
Soweto for themselves. They'd always been strong believers
in not discriminating against anyone, so it must have been
confronting to see apartheid up close. I remembered my trip
to South Africa in 1990 when Mandela was freed from jail
and became president four years later. I hoped it brought joy
to everyone in Soweto.

The day I started Year 7 at Riverside High School, I was as
anxious as I'd been when our plane circled over Mauritius.
I'd heard there were tough kids—kids who *smoked* and
initiated newcomers by flushing their heads in the toilet. My
anxiety turned out to be unwarranted and soon gave way to
something more pleasant: I fell in love for the first time. Her
name was Joanne Hunter. She was friendly, talkative and
smart, had blonde hair and usually wore a blazer.

In Year 7, we held hands and sometimes kissed. After
school, we would talk on the phone. At our house, the old
landline phone was next to the TV, so Joanne and I would
chat until someone inevitably yelled 'Get off the phone!' and
we had to reluctantly hang up after just an hour or two.
Joanne and I lasted a year as a couple, which is a long time
when you're twelve years old.

There were other girls I felt close to in high school, but
none had as strong an impact on me as Joanne. While I was
jealous when she later went out with one of my mates, we
stayed friends.

In early high school, I had many friends, including my cousin Maree. My three closest mates were Tim Sutton, Rob Knight and Malcolm Leach. Someone once described us as 'the fab four', which felt like a nice compliment.

Family was central to my life, though. Mum was in much better health and was teaching at St Anthony's. Dad was enjoying teaching auto electrics at TAFE. Mark and I had our own friends at school but, as a family, we still went away regularly for weekends and holidays.

Instead of going to Ulverstone, the family summer holidays had switched to camping at Ransons Beach on the north-east coast. We also went on more ambitious walking trips to Pine Valley—Mum hiked in with us one Easter—and had holidays at Frenchmans Cap, Bicheno, St Helens and Coles Bay. Like just about everywhere in Tassie, these were places of exceptional natural beauty.

At school, it gradually became obvious that I was short-sighted. Even though I knew it was a problem, I was dead against wearing glasses. I imagined myself as a pretty cool guy who played a lot of sport, and pretty cool guys in Launceston in 1981, as I saw it, did not wear glasses.

I often sat at the back of the class, which was also what pretty cool guys in Launceston did, but couldn't see the blackboard, so I had to ask whoever was sitting next to me if I could copy their work. When an eye test confirmed that my vision was terrible, my parents knew it was time to act. Dad took me to an optometrist in the city to get—the *horror!*—my first pair of glasses, and I was mortified.

As we left, Dad told me to put them on. As soon as I did, a girl from school who I was keen on walked past with her dad. She didn't say anything but I was embarrassed. My image of myself as a hip character went out the window.

Even though short-sightedness must have affected how I caught a footy or a cricket ball, I would only wear my glasses in class. Outside, I would rather be short-sighted than be mistaken for a nerd.

The next year, there was salvation when I learned a friend's brother wore contact lenses. My parents bought them for me and my life changed. I felt more confident and they helped me when I was playing sport. But for years I continued being self-conscious whenever I had to wear glasses.

Outside school hours, I'd ride around Launceston on my bike, a red Malvern Star. In summer, I regularly rode with the other members of the fab four up to Cataract Gorge, near the centre of town, to swim. The water was never really cold in summer but it was incredibly refreshing on a hot day as we dived in and swam across the gorge. We'd get out and jump in again off the rocks. We'd get a pie or a sandwich from the kiosk, which my friend Rob's mum ran. We'd explore up the river. We'd play cricket. I loved it there.

Outside the fab four, I made a new friend in David Grant, who came to Riverside High from another school and was a brilliant football player—way better than me. In the mornings, David helped on his dad's milk round, which meant he was really fit. We'd kick a footy, play table tennis and catch frogs at the school dam for no other reason than it was fun. At one time we were keeping twenty green frogs in a tub covered with a fly screen; we fed them until, one by one, they escaped. He became one of my closest mates until his parents split up and he moved to another school just before Year 10. I felt like I'd lost a real friend.

David went on to play for St Kilda in the VFL and AFL, clocking up almost 200 games alongside such legends as Tony Lockett, Nicky Winmar, Robert Harvey and Nathan Burke. He was named in the All-Australian team—an honour for the season's best players—in 1991. I saw him once after a St Kilda game when we were both in our twenties, then didn't see him again until 2022, when I ran into him in a car park in Launceston. We recognised each other immediately and have talked on the phone since about our childhood memories. We laughed about catching those frogs, then being outsmarted by them.

––––––––

Despite not studying much, I was a good student and came to expect excellent marks when we had exams. In maths, Daniel Kirkham and I were nearly always the top two, but that changed suddenly when we had to learn and apply algebraic formulas. In my first exam on the topic, I scored just 55 per cent. I was upset; my adolescent ego was bruised.

I realised I had to start studying—if not all the time, at least strategically. While I tried to downplay it, deep inside I desperately wanted to succeed. It helped that Mark was two years ahead of me at school. He had figured out how everything worked at Riverside High and helped me to find my way, giving me his notes when he'd already studied the subjects I was doing.

My parents never pushed Mark and me, but I was always ambitious, whether in schoolwork or sport. At school, I was more drawn to kids who had fun and were good at sport than I was to the 'smart' kids. My role models in early high school were all sporting stars: Hawthorn players Leigh Matthews, Peter Knights and Don Scott, and champion basketballer Ian Davies, who played for Launceston and was top scorer for the Australian Boomers at the Moscow Olympics in 1980. I competed in all sorts of sports: athletics, squash, swimming, volleyball, cricket, cross-country running, basketball, social soccer, touch football (rugby league) and Aussie Rules. I loved Aussie Rules so much that, for a while, I was playing for both Riverside High and the Launceston Blues, Dad's old team, on weekends.

Launceston often had heavy fogs during winter. Being on the Tamar River, we would regularly walk through thick fog on the way to school in winter. Playing for the school on Saturday mornings, we sometimes couldn't see from one end of the ground to the other. The two goal umpires had to meet in the middle at the end of every quarter to work out the score.

It was also freezing, with temperatures usually in the single digits and sometimes down to −5°C. We would get very cold waiting for the ball to emerge from the fog down the other end of the field. When it did, it was hard trying to mark with frozen fingers. Luckily, I often played ruck rover or wing, and all the running I had to do helped me warm up.

On Sundays, I would back up to play for the Blues and, in the early years, we regularly won premierships. While I was capable, I was far from the best player in either of my two teams. I was a late developer as a teenager—tall and skinny—and my coordination was less than ideal. In some sports, I was better in primary school than I was in high school. But I really liked playing in a team, and I loved the way everyone worked together to succeed. The camaraderie—bonding as friends—sometimes felt more important than winning. While I wanted to win, I enjoyed playing even when we didn't have a strong team. I learned a lesson that has carried on into my adult life: building a team is an important part of success. It's as true in medical research and clinical care as it is in footy.

Dad always came to my games to watch from the sidelines, giving me advice before we started and in the sheds at half-time. 'Focus on the ball,' he'd urge. 'Lead out more.' Mum would come along, too, but she usually stayed in the car and read a book.

Like most teenagers, I did my share of what legendary Australian singer Paul Kelly calls the 'dumb things'. I was fourteen when I went camping at Badger Head, on the north coast, with a group of mates during the September school holidays. The weather was awful—cold and rainy—and the surf was crappy. One day some older guys who could drive turned up. We took turns lying on the roof of their car as it sped along the beach while the driver swerved to try to make us fall off.

We were so cold and wet—our tent had fallen down—that Tim Sutton, three other friends and I broke into a YMCA hut that was used for school trips. I knew it was stupid but we wanted somewhere dry to sleep. When a supervisor saw what we'd done the next day, Tim and I had to front up to the head of the YMCA to get a stern dressing-down.

While I'd been told off before at home, this was the first time I'd been chewed out by someone I didn't know. I was ashamed and embarrassed, and I felt even worse when I saw that my parents were disappointed in me. I should have argued against doing it. It was a turning point in my young life: I realised I had to stand up for myself when something didn't feel right.

I kept it quiet from Mum and Dad when I first went out drinking, aged fifteen, which was common in Launceston at the time. But whenever I told them I was going out, they wanted me to let them know when I'd be home. Once, when I was sixteen, I'd been at my friend Judy Harrison's house and we'd been innocently talking for hours so I didn't get back till 3 a.m. Dad had stayed up waiting and was upset. I didn't like worrying him.

So it was a relief later when my parents and relatives excavated under the house, giving us a new rumpus room, a downstairs bedroom for me and an extra bathroom. A garage door next to my new bedroom let me sneak in, and I could come and go as I wanted.

In Year 9 at Riverside High School, my cousin and close friend Maree and I were voted head prefects. It didn't feel like a huge deal to me so I just mentioned it in passing to Mum as I headed out the door to kick a footy. She was proud but kept telling her friends, 'He just told me in a throwaway line.' I guess it would have been nice to let her enjoy the moment instead of disappearing into the afternoon and not getting back until dinnertime.

I was pleased in my own way but being head prefect meant speaking in public, which I'd never done before. I was nervous about having to make speeches at assembly and I had to practise so I'd get better at it. It was good training for when I had to speak at medical conferences later in life. Maree was a better public speaker than me. But the more I did it, the more comfortable I felt.

On Riverside High's birthday, I had to join fellow prefects Tim Sutton, Cam Matthews and Dan Witte in singing 'Happy Birthday' over the speaker system to the whole school. Some others baulked but, as head prefect, I had to join in. It was probably easier than public speaking but must have been painful for everyone listening. We were lousy singers. Lucky the school only had one birthday a year.

With our parents continuing to encourage Mark and me to get part-time jobs, I found my best one yet. It was three shifts a week—Thursday night, Friday night and Saturday morning—at a Roelf Vos supermarket, which was virtually across the road from our house.

Vos was quite a character. After being involved in the Dutch resistance during World War II, he arrived in Tasmania in the 1950s and built a business that started with the north's first self-service grocery store. He became well known for his low-budget TV ads that promised shopping would be 'a sheer delight'.

At the supermarket, the boys stacked the shelves and packed customers' groceries in recycled boxes or bags while the girls, including Maree, were on the checkouts. It was a job that gave me some welcome independence when I was paid—in cash, with a proper payslip—every week. I bought sports gear, records, tapes, Wagon Wheels—a favourite treat—and lollies.

Looking back now, I can see that it was a job that taught me about working with a boss, responsibility, the need to communicate well with the people you work with and the value of money. I put $8 into my savings account every week. I was looking forward to buying a car when I was old enough to drive.

I loved music and, despite my poor singing, went through a brief stage of dreaming about being a rock star. All I lacked was the talent and the good looks. I started learning how to play guitar from my cousin Michael but didn't get too far. I liked seeing top bands, though, when they played in Launceston. I saw Australian Crawl at the Princess Theatre and INXS at the annual Basin Concert at Cataract Gorge. I had a record player and a lot of scratched records. In my mid teens, my favourite band was Midnight Oil.

With rock stardom out of the question, I had a week of work experience with the draftsmen at the Repco car-parts factory. I quickly decided that working in a factory wasn't for me. I wanted to do something I really enjoyed, and something that made a difference.

———————

In Year 10, I decided to be a doctor.

After my mum's health struggles, I wanted to help people. I figured I got on well with just about everyone, which I thought would be a good quality in a doctor. I was also confident I had the academic ability to get into medicine at uni. I told one of my friends, who said, 'God, you'll have to go to uni for a long time.'

'I don't care,' I replied—and I meant it.

There were some doctors in and around our family who I liked, but they weren't the main inspiration for my decision. They included two uncles: Phil, who was a junior doctor in Launceston while I was in primary school then became a GP in Moruya on the NSW south coast, and Tony, a paediatrician in Canberra. My parents had a good friend who was a local GP—Don Grimes, who lived around the corner. He quit medicine and became a senator for Tasmania in 1974.

After breaking my finger and falling out of a tree in South Africa, I managed to stay away from doctors as a teenager. But the more I heard about medicine, the more I liked the sound of it. I'd see on the TV news reports about doctors helping injured sports stars, and I'd observed friends and their parents being successfully treated when they were ill. I'd seen how valuable doctors were when my dad had a melanoma cut out and a hiatus hernia repaired, and when

Mum had a hysterectomy. The medical system had done a lot for the community I knew.

I think I was kind-hearted as a teenager—a quality I hope I still have—and wanted to help people in a practical way in my life. What initially appealed was the idea of working closely with a community as a country GP. But I later learned, in medical school, that the job was changing: GPs were referring more patients to specialists as medicine became more complicated, and they seemed to be doing less surgical and other practical procedures, which were things that appealed to me. So I became interested in specialising in one field.

There was a divide among my friends at around this age. Some of the boys, even the smart ones, left school after the School Certificate at the end of Year 10 to find a job.

But most of the girls among my friends continued to Year 12 so they could get a Higher School Certificate. Some went to TAFE to become teachers. Others wanted to go to uni—including Joanne Hunter, my first love, who became a clinical psychologist.

It didn't strike me until years later that, whatever they did after finishing school, nobody thought about leaving Tassie. The jobs were usually local and, in 1982, there was only one uni destination: the University of Tasmania in Hobart.

In Year 10, I won Riverside High's Scott–Kilvert Prize, awarded to a student who demonstrated the qualities shown by Ewen Scott and David Kilvert, the Riverside teacher and student who had died at Cradle Mountain in the 1960s: 'unselfishness, a spirit of mateship, comradeship, courage, loyalty to a cause and dedication to a task'. I was pleased to be recognised and, loving the outdoors like they did and having been to where they died, I could see it was a significant award. But it felt like I'd just been doing my best as head prefect—organising activities and supporting kids—rather than anything that involved their kind of comradeship or courage.

My studies were going well, too, so I also won the Academic Proficiency Prize and a distinction in the Australian Mathematics Competition.

Then it was time to leave Riverside High.

In the Tassie education system, students had to go to a dedicated matriculation college to study for the Higher School Certificate. Mine was Launceston Community College in town. Before starting, I had to choose my subjects for Years 11 and 12, which is where it helped having a brother two years ahead of me at school.

A mate of Mark's, Andrew 'Spatzy' Spillane, had wanted to study medicine but was given the wrong advice about the subjects he needed. As a result, he was only accepted into medical school when other students pulled out. So Spatzy, who later became a brilliant surgeon at Melanoma Institute Australia, told me which subjects to choose. I went for the right mix of physics, chemistry, biology and mathematics, supplemented with computer studies, English and accounting.

My parents backed my plan to become a doctor, especially Mum, whose dad hadn't allowed her to finish university. But to get into medicine, I needed to do well, so I cut back on the sport I was playing to focus on my studies. I still went to parties on the weekend and played basketball for Sanyo City in an adult competition in the evenings. But I gave up competitive footy and just kicked a ball on the oval at lunchtimes.

I settled into a routine of studying most nights, always with the radio on. I listened to Launceston's cool pop stations, 7LA and 7EX.

When I was in Year 11, Mark went to uni to study engineering, and I became the only kid in the house. Times were changing.

Launceston Community College was terrific. I loved how social and grown-up it was. At Riverside High, you had to wear a school uniform, there were very young kids and it was regimented. There were strict rules: we could only go to certain parts of the school grounds; we had to go to assemblies.

Now, school was much more relaxed. We didn't have to wear a uniform. There wasn't a roll that was checked in the mornings. We could turn up for as much of the day as we wanted; some people only had part of their schedule filled up. If we didn't turn up, no one chased us.

Socially, too, it felt like we were now young adults. And while there were top students from other high schools at Launceston Community College, I was still strong academically.

While I'd already been going out drinking with friends, now we sometimes went to a pub near the school at lunchtime to play pool and have a beer. I was only seventeen but the teachers who were there on their lunch break never seemed to mind that we were drinking. Underage drinking appeared to be an accepted part of the culture at the time.

One night in Year 11, I was at a party with friends when there was a troubling incident. I hadn't drunk much when two older guys came up to us and started acting strangely and laughing weirdly. They were drunk.

Out of nowhere, one of them threw a punch at me. I stepped back and he missed. My friends and I all bolted and these guys chased me; I must have stood out because I was tall and skinny. Fortunately I was a good runner. I was also terrified about being beaten up, which made me even faster. I got away. With a friend who'd also run off, I snuck through the garage door at my house and kept the lights off until we were sure they'd given up.

I was never a kid who got into fights and I was scared. This guy was stupid for throwing a punch like that. Years later, I learned how often coward punches can be fatal. If there was a lesson there, it was to trust my instincts. I knew from how these guys were acting that something bad would happen. I was lucky that I stepped back.

In Year 12, we went on a school trip to the University of Tasmania, where I'd been hoping to study medicine. I met the medical school's head of administration and asked him about the admission requirements. He told me the required subjects, how the entry score was determined and the cut-off marks for the past five years.

Thanks to Spatzy, I'd done the right Year 11 subjects and passed with some of the highest marks in the state. In the

Tassie system, Year 11 and Year 12 subjects counted equally towards our Higher School Certificate, so I was already way higher than the cut-off. That meant I just had to pass the last compulsory subject in Year 12—Biology B—to get into medicine. There was none of the stress that Year 12 students in other states had, with everything resting on their final exams.

But I must have taken it easier than I thought in Year 12 because my accounting teacher was disappointed I didn't top the state in the subject. And my maths teacher was upset I didn't study a subject called extension maths. My logic was that I didn't like maths that much and preferred having a social life to spending extra hours studying. And importantly, I didn't need those marks to get into medicine.

In Year 12, my friend Mark 'Baldy' Baldock was voted president of the student council and I became vice president. We used our influence to endorse dances, fetes and other events where our fellow students could enjoy themselves.

Baldy, who was a fun guy, wanted to study medicine, too. On the university application form, there was the option of nominating pharmacy as a second choice. I didn't tick that box. If I didn't get into medicine, my fallback plan was to take a year off and go travelling.

———

Before thinking too far ahead about uni, I got my driver's licence at seventeen. My Uncle Phil sold me his car, an old

Ford ute, for $500. And, being seventeen, I loved doing burnouts in it.

Dad had encouraged me to do a course in basic car maintenance, so I knew how a car worked and how to look after it, as well as gaining a skill that came in useful a few years later: how to hotwire a car.

I also learned that being on the road in Tassie could be dangerous.

Just after Christmas in 1983, we'd been bushwalking and camping with some of our relatives at Cape Pillar in southern Tassie. It was a fabulous place—except there were too many snakes—and we'd seen the first three yachts dicing for line honours around Tasman Island in the Sydney to Hobart Yacht Race. When we finished the trip, Dad and Mark shared the driving back home.

Mum had stayed in Hobart, where we'd celebrated Christmas, so she drove to a spot to meet us about 10 p.m. I hopped into her Toyota Corolla to get back to Launceston. Before long, I could tell Mum was getting tired, so I asked a couple of times if she wanted me to drive. She kept saying no because I couldn't go faster than 80 kilometres an hour on my L-plates, which meant it would take us longer to get home.

We were almost at Campbell Town when Mum fell asleep. The Corolla started to run off the road to the left; she over-corrected as she woke up and it veered off to the right. The car rolled three and a half times, luckily avoiding trees and power poles, and ended up on its roof, down a slope and in a paddock.

We were upside down but, with our seatbelts on, we weren't injured. I was anxious, though, that petrol was leaking and the car would blow up. After winding down the windows, we scrambled out.

Mark, who was driving behind us, saw the accident, woke Dad up and pulled over.

They checked we weren't injured, then, with the help of other drivers who had stopped, rolled the Corolla back onto its wheels and pushed it back to the road. Mum and I were both shaken up, so Dad and Mark drove the two cars home. It only struck me later how fortunate we'd been.

Nine months later, I was driving my ute back from a surfing trip at Tam O'Shanter Bay on the north coast. I dropped off a mate, Guy Jetson, at his family's farm, his mum put on a nice meal, then I set off for Launceston.

At dusk, I was driving down a winding mountain road, just past Scottsdale, in the rain—stupidly wearing glasses with an old prescription instead of my contact lenses; the glasses were propped up with rubber bands and a battery on my nose, so I could see as well as possible. I was driving faster than I should have been in the conditions.

Rounding a corner, I suddenly saw a log truck driving very slowly in front. I hit the brakes, the wheels locked up and the ute slid into the underside of the truck. A metal pole ripped through the car roof close to my head.

While the driver surely must have felt a jolt, the truck kept crawling down the mountain. My heart was pounding. Had my car not hit the truck, it could have skidded over the edge of a cliff. I checked the damage: besides the torn roof, the windscreen was cracked but I could still see through it. One side of the ute was banged up.

After about fifteen minutes, I slowly drove home. It was a lonely area so I didn't see any other cars till I was close to Launceston. I was so, so lucky—for the second time in less than a year.

My parents were away for the weekend so, at a time before mobile phones, I didn't tell them about the accident until they made it home. I was embarrassed about it. When they heard, they were shocked to hear how close I'd come to dying. But there was only love from them, not anger—even though that might have been justified.

Dad and I fixed the damage to the roof but repairing the dents on the side cost more money than I had. After we banged out what we could, the rest of the dents had to stay for as long as I had the ute.

A boy in the year ahead of me at school, a talented footballer, was later killed in a car crash. A few years on, six youths were killed in a car crash with a log truck at Swansea on the east coast. They were reminders of just how fortunate I'd been. I became a more sensible driver, determined to make the most of my life.

When it was time to sit for exams at the end of the year, I was already carrying those strong Year 11 results towards the Higher School Certificate. If everything went well, I'd move away from Launceston for the first time.

I was ready.

4

MOVING INTO MEDICINE

While waiting for my exam results at the end of Year 12, I took a working holiday in Queensland with Mark, who was doing work experience with the construction company now known as Lendlease.

The trip had a rocky start when I took Mark's car, a hotted-up old Falcon sedan, on the overnight car ferry to Melbourne. The seats near me were full of bikies who stayed up all night drinking. I hardly had any sleep before I met Mark, who'd flown from Hobart to Melbourne. We then spent two days driving more than 1600 kilometres to Brisbane, eating at pubs and staying in motels along the way.

Lendlease had a house that we could rent for the bargain price of $20 a week. Because it would soon be knocked down to build apartments, there was no furniture and half the windows didn't have any glass. Being poor students, we hired only the furniture we thought was essential and slept on mattresses on the floor.

Brisbane in summer was a new experience. During the first night, I woke up with cockroaches crawling over me. But living in such a ramshackle house had advantages: when some mates from Tassie visited, we played cricket indoors, knowing we didn't have to worry about smashing any windows.

I found a job as an attendant in an underground car park. It was the kind of place where drivers left their keys so we could shuffle around cars to get them in and out. Sometimes I manned the ticket booth, which I liked—except when drivers were upset about the price of parking. I had to politely point out a sign that showed how much it cost before they entered.

Being in Queensland over summer was a chance to go surfing. While I loved surfing in Tassie, I wasn't very good. I couldn't really stand up on a board. But when I visited my cousin Dave on the Gold Coast, he took me to the point break at Kirra and I learned how to surf properly. I was so proud catching my first wave—paddling into position, feeling the power of the water, getting to my feet and surfing into shore, endorphins flowing. It was exhilarating!

We sometimes surfed with a mate of Dave's called Tank. I later learned there was a photo of Tank and me surfing at Broadbeach that the airline Ansett used on the front cover of its magazine and on posters. When I asked about it at an Ansett office, they let me take a poster from their front window.

I visited the Sunshine Coast a couple of times, first with Mark then with some mates, staying in a caravan park at Coolum. It was a magic place, with a beach lifestyle that I really enjoyed.

I found out my exam results in January. They were as good as I'd been hoping and I was accepted into medicine at the University of Tasmania. I couldn't have asked for a better Year 12 reference than the one written by the principal of Launceston Community College, who said I had 'a keen enquiring mind' and was 'strongly self-motivated', with 'a marked capacity for hard work and perseverance'. He added that I was 'a very cheerful, co-operative and sensible young man' who 'enjoys life, has a good sense of humour and is both well liked and respected by his fellow students'. I was 'a person of absolute integrity'.

When I look at it now, that sums up what I was trying to be—especially the references to being self-motivated, having integrity and enjoying life. I hoped that Mum and Dad were proud of a son they had done so much for.

My friend Baldy missed out on medicine, but was accepted into pharmacy as his second option. It turned out to be a triumphant move: he became a successful pharmacist who owned a series of practices. Years later, Baldy switched to medicine and became a GP in Hobart. There was one other boy in my year at high school, Martin Wade, who had wanted to study medicine, too. He got in and became a dermatologist, and was later based in London.

I told the two guys I worked with at the car park that I was heading home to study medicine and was surprised by their reaction. It seemed strange that they had a new respect for me: the kid from Tassie was going to be a doctor!

Mark and I drove the old Falcon south again, and we had a couple of weeks in Launceston before heading to Hobart. I was excited about leaving home—being more independent—and going to uni. It would be an adventure.

———

I moved into Christ College, where Mark had stayed for his first two years at uni (he'd since moved into a share house with friends). The location was convenient: the medical school was just down the hill. While it was the first Tasmanian uni residential college to accept both men and women, my year was very male dominated.

Initially, I found the social side of uni life more exciting than studying medicine. I started playing football again, for both university and college teams. I made new friends as I joined a busy program of social activities that included parties and intercollege basketball and netball. I even joined a scavenger hunt, driving around Hobart to find answers to cryptic clues.

While the name sounded religious, Christ College was a wild place. The second- and third-year students delighted in initiating first-years with pranks and a running race that involved eating a cold meat pie, sculling a warm beer and other stomach-churning acts designed to make the newcomers vomit.

College life seemed like a constant party, with an excuse to drink almost every night. While determined to be a doctor, I also liked having fun and fitting in. But even so, I quickly became uneasy about some of the behaviour in college and the fact there was pressure on first-years to do things we didn't want to do.

Some kids drank heavily and did stupid things. While I should have spoken up more than I did, I felt secure enough about who I was, even at eighteen, to avoid the worst of the boozy blokeyness.

I also had almost 40 contact hours a week in medicine, which was a lot more than some of the biggest party animals at the college.

In first term, despite a heavy workload that went more deeply into physics and chemistry than anything I'd studied in year 12, there was time to get to know the other first-year medical students. There were 48 of us. Two-thirds were women. More were from public than private schools. They were an interesting group.

Most of them didn't have their own cars, so when we visited hospitals in Hobart to see how patients were being treated, I packed five of us onto the single bench seat of my ute—illegally and, in retrospect, not very intelligently given my past car accidents. Happily, we avoided becoming patients ourselves.

My nanna—Mum's mum—lived in Hobart and had a hat shop in the Cat and Fiddle Arcade, then later in the Bank Arcade. It was a landmark for medical students. Teaching neurology, Dr Keith Millingen always directed them to get a hatpin from Nanna's shop so they could test patients' visual fields. She wouldn't have expected that business when she opened the shop.

Nanna had me around every week for a meal that was always delicious. Sometimes we were joined by relatives who I'd visited in Johannesburg—my Aunty Rose, Uncle Alan and their sons Chris and Andy. When the boys were faced with two years of compulsory military service in South Africa, the family had moved from Johannesburg to just south of Hobart.

For all my illusions about being cool in high school, I never cared much about fashion at uni. I had two pairs of tracksuit pants that I teamed with a flannelette shirt, footy socks and sandshoes. I bought a long woollen coat for $5 from an op shop and wore it everywhere in winter.

While I passed first year, four students out of the 48 failed and had to leave. Four older students switching to medicine after another degree took their place. I should have recognised that the students who'd failed had the same dream of being a doctor as me, but I took it for granted that I'd keep getting through.

Mum was adamant that I shouldn't get a part-time job during term time—she wanted me to focus on my studies—so I left work until the holidays. Labouring jobs were the best option to earn money quickly.

For my first summer break, Dad found me work with a Launceston construction company. We mostly built roads but, as I regularly pointed out to my kids in later life, I also helped make a new car park at the supermarket I worked at in Riverside, across the road from my parents' house. Just as there had been at college, there was a period of initiation on worksites, with the crew making me sit away from them at meal breaks. Once I was through that, I became part of the family. After the strange reaction I'd had from my car park workmates in Brisbane, I didn't tell them I was studying medicine.

————

At the start of my second year at uni, I met Marie Ayre, an arts student who later specialised in psychology. I'd gone surfing at Clifton Beach with some friends, including Baldy, who was keen on her—and more popular with women than me—and he'd organised for our respective friends to meet at a pub. Marie and I talked, hit it off and started going out.

Marie became my first real girlfriend. She was friendly, sensitive, caring and always seemed happy. We fell in love.

Around this time, at the encouragement of my college-football teammates, I joined another side that our coach, former Melbourne Demons player John Clennett, had taken over: Hutchins School Old Boys. They played in the top amateur league in Hobart. That meant my second year at uni was much better than my first—I'd made new friends, I was having a fantastic social life with Marie, and I was playing for a strong footy team.

Marie was eighteen and I was nineteen—very much teenagers—and we would trade pranks. It started with her playfully stealing a poster off my college room wall of *Sale of the Century* model Judy Green. To get Marie back, I climbed up the outside of Marie's two-storey house at Lower Sandy Bay, with my friend Tim 'Led' Ledingham, who I'd known since we'd played school sport against each other in Launceston, urging me on from the footpath. Before I made it inside, I saw a police car down the road jamming on the brakes and reversing towards us. A cop charged up; he thought he'd interrupted a burglary, until Marie's house-mate vouched for me.

When the cop left, I smuggled some of Marie's clothes back to my room. She and her friends responded by painting my beloved white ute with animals and other designs in bright colours. So I hotwired her car one night and parked it in the middle of the university quadrangle, where cars weren't allowed. She had to drive it out the next morning, as amused students and lecturers looked on.

Then Marie brought around a cake she'd made for me. I was suspicious and was right to be—the ingredients included a box of laxatives. I didn't want anything to do with it but one of the guys from college, Brad, unfortunately ate enough to suffer the consequences. We decided the pranking war had gone far enough.

Marie and I sometimes headed out of Hobart to go camping, or to visit her family in Queenstown on weekends and during uni holidays. One freakish day, it snowed in Hobart. A friend and I took the fins off our surfboards and rode them down a hill. The next day we went surfing so we could get photos of ourselves in the water while there was snow on the beach.

At uni that year, I found studying physiology fascinating: learning how the body worked, all the systems—nervous, cardiovascular, respiratory, digestive, endocrine and urinary— and how they fitted together. Biochemistry I thought was fine but less exciting. Anatomy was interesting but required rote learning—all those muscles, bones, nerves and blood vessels— which was hard when there was so much else going on in my life.

I realised just before the end-of-year exams that I hadn't done enough work. I was suddenly anxious that I wouldn't get through to third year.

A quarter of the year failed and had to do second year again, including the subjects they'd passed. Some of the students who failed deserved to get through more than I did, but I managed to pass. I hadn't done the work so it must have been good exam technique—and luck—that got me over the line.

That near miss changed me. I realised I had to grow up if I wanted to be a doctor.

I'd never had so much going on in my life before—living away from home, a girlfriend, so many friends, a full social life, a good footy team. I was used to doing well academic- ally without having to apply myself too much. So nearly failing was definitely a wake-up call.

Summer gave me time to visit my parents, who had been staying in a caravan during the year while building a new house at Legana, just up the road from Riverside. It was also time to get a job.

I found work shovelling and raking around concrete pours at the Cornwall colliery in the small town of Fingal. The worst part was travelling from Launceston every day, five of us in a car. The two guys who owned the car were heavy drinkers and I hated how fast they drove back at night.

After Christmas, I found a much more enjoyable job: working with my cousin Johnny, who had a landscape-gardening business in Launceston. He drove a bobcat while I shovelled. When I was out celebrating my 21st birthday, I called myself 'the human bobcat'.

It was a good-natured crew that also included my Uncle Bern, Dad's brother. One day I took Bern's lunch while he wasn't looking and hoisted it to the top of a flagpole. The rest of us sat quietly eating our own lunches, acting normally, while Bern wandered around looking for his. He was baffled until everyone burst out laughing. Later, we had a brush with Tassie royalty when we worked on the yard of supermarket king Roelf Vos.

———

Back at uni, I moved out of college, which took away a lot of the distractions that had almost caused me to fail the previous year. I'd been used to having breakfast, lunch and dinner with friends every day and joining too many social activities. This year I had to focus on studying.

My new home was a weatherboard house in Sandy Bay that I shared with Susie Welch, a pharmacy student who I'd known since infants school in Launceston, and Josh Carmody, a law student from Sydney. When Josh went back to Sydney, Jim Finlay, a close friend from college and football, moved in.

Susie was a caring person who was very organised, so it was a fun household. Her parents, who owned the house, generously kept the rent low and didn't charge us when we left for uni holidays. The only drawback was that the house had an outside shower and toilet. When the temperature was below zero on winter mornings, it was an icy trip to the backyard. It took a brutally long time for the water to warm up for a shower.

With a less hectic social life, I focused on studying. Marie and I would sometimes study together at my place. We were spending almost every night with each other.

Studying pathology in third and fourth year, I found an inspiring group of teachers. Professor Konrad Muller and senior lecturers John McArdle and David Challis brilliantly explained what pathology was and why it mattered. By analysing tissue through a microscope and other techniques, pathologists, as they described it, were the bridge between science and physiology, revealing how and why a disease affected patients, their prognosis and how they should be treated. So many of us found these teachers inspiring that the percentage of medical students who became pathologists in my time at the uni was higher than at any other medical school in the country.

I didn't see pathology as a career at this stage, though. After moving on from wanting to be a GP in the country, I'd decided to be a specialist but hadn't decided on a field yet. I seemed to be inspired by almost every specialty I got to know.

I'd settled into a study routine that meant I made it through third year without the fear of failing I'd had in second year. After some labouring jobs at the start of the summer holidays, I set off with Marie on a huge trip after Christmas. We took buses and trains all the way from Melbourne to the Gold Coast and Sunshine Coast, with stops along the way in Canberra, the NSW south coast and Sydney.

In fourth year, we did all our subjects at Royal Hobart Hospital's clinical school, including surgery, internal medicine (such as cardiology, neurology and gastroenterology), pathology and microbiology. I found it incredibly stimulating and learned valuable practical skills for treating patients.

I loved working in the emergency department where, for the first time, I was able to really help people in a crisis. It was an adrenaline rush and it felt like I handled the pressure well. I thought about specialising in emergency medicine.

In the next summer holidays, Marie and I went even further by train than we had the previous year. We made it all the way to Cairns, then spent a month hopping towns south, camping as we went, all the way to the Whitsundays. We spent so much time in the sun that, before too long, I had a tan and my hair was bleached blond. At the time, I thought it was a good look. Decades later, I realised how much damage I'd done to my skin. In my early thirties, I had to get treatment for a basal cell carcinoma—a slow-growing skin cancer—on my forehead. Despite all the time I spent in the sun, that BCC over two decades later has been my only skin cancer. When I began working in melanoma, I realised how lucky I'd been.

———

In my fifth year at uni, during a term at Launceston General Hospital, I was doing a temporary stint with a local football team when there was a real 'is there a doctor in the house?' moment. A player went down injured, with his leg alarmingly crooked. It didn't take a medical degree to diagnose what was wrong—a broken tibia and fibula. I helped keep him as calm as possible until an ambulance took him to hospital.

As medical students, we would go out with ambulances on emergency calls. There was one extraordinary afternoon when we were called to a house where a boy of three or four was unconscious—apparently dead—after falling into a backyard pool. The parents were distraught. The dad was angry; it seemed like he blamed himself for not supervising the boy around the pool. Working quickly and without panic, the ambos were able to resuscitate the boy. While he was crying, he seemed to be back to his normal self. The parents were so grateful and, watching on, I felt their joy. Everyone celebrated. I knew it already but seeing a child brought back from the brink drove home the value of what I was studying.

Throughout fifth and sixth year, we were rotated around hospitals in Tassie: I did obstetrics and gynaecology in Latrobe, near Devonport; and internal medicine, surgery and psychiatry in Launceston. I also did two weeks of GP training with my Uncle Phil at Moruya in New South Wales, then three weeks in Hobart with a doctor I met in Queenstown through Marie's dad. I saw all the hard work that GPs did for their communities, how varied it was and the importance of their relationship with patients.

Halfway through fifth year there was a blow: Marie broke up with me. I was heartbroken, but I had to accept it. I'd been away on rotations for months at a time; she'd almost finished her degree and had her own plans. I was down for weeks and tried to distract myself with studying and sport.

For my elective term before sixth year, I decided to go to England. That meant I had to find a hospital or a medical clinic that would take me for what was effectively five weeks of work experience. I was accepted at a gastroenterology department at Royal Berkshire Hospital in Reading, west of London.

When I arrived and met the supervising doctor, he signed my form and said I didn't need to turn up to the hospital every day and I should line up some holidays. After moving into the nurses' accommodation, I came to work more than he was expecting, but I also took his advice and went travelling.

I had long weekends visiting uni friends doing their elective terms in London, and relatives in Cornwall—home of the original Scolyers. I was puzzled: it wasn't clear why these relatives, Rod and Mary Allan, had a different surname. And I couldn't find any other Scolyers when I checked a local registry, so I was no help supplementing the family tree.

I also went to Scotland to visit my Uncle Rod, Mum's brother, and his wife Liz, who lived in Edinburgh; and two classmates from medical school, Steph Dean and Suzie Smallbane, who were doing their elective terms in Glasgow. My Edinburgh relatives drove all of us around beautiful Scotland for four days.

I tried to ring my parents from a phone booth every week while I was in the UK. Well and truly settled in the new house in Legana, they were now planning an early retirement.

When my Reading placement finished, I went travelling around Europe with Steph and Suzie for four weeks. We were joined by a young American woman, a ski-instructor-turned-backpacker, who we met at the start of our trip. The four of us bought 28-day Eurail passes and either slept on overnight trains or stayed at youth hostels. Our backpacker lifestyle extended to eating as cheaply as possible—often just cheese on a bread roll for lunch and meals in hostels when they offered it.

We went to some amazing places . . . Rome, Cinque Terre, Portofino, Paris, Nice, Lyon, Andorra, the Loire Valley, Barcelona, Amsterdam, Munich, Zürich, Salzburg, Venice. I was blown away by their beauty, how different they were from anywhere I'd known, and the incredible sense of history in Europe. Just as I'd done in South Africa when I was twelve,

I learned there were very different ways of living to what I'd known. It sparked my interest in seeing more of the world.

It was January 1990 and the Eastern Bloc had just opened up—and was cheap to visit—so we went to Budapest, another stunning place. We had the full backpacker experience when we changed money with dodgy-looking guys behind buildings.

Wherever we went around Europe, it was common to arrive on a train in the middle of a city and get mobbed by touts offering cheap accommodation. Like every other Aussie backpacker in Europe, we relied on a well-used copy of *Lonely Planet* for advice on accommodation, food and travel. We had a brilliant trip.

Back in Hobart in March for my final year of medical studies, I moved out of Susie's place to split my time between the clinical school student accommodation at the hospital and a tiny spare room in 'Led' Ledingham's share house. Throughout medical school, I continued playing football for Hutchins School Old Boys—mostly first grade, but sometimes seconds, depending on how well I was playing—and continued a social life that included numerous black-tie functions. They'd been a constant throughout university—at college, medical school, 21st birthdays and sporting clubs—and they were fun events.

Not surprisingly, given what was at stake, the exams at the end of sixth year were stressful. I had to come up with a diagnosis and recommend management for Tasmania's first HIV-positive patient, and another patient who was psychotic.

For a medical student under pressure in an exam, the challenge was coming up with long-term management plans.

Before the results came out, I had to nominate where I'd like to work as an intern—a junior doctor's first job out of medical school. I decided to stay in Hobart. When I passed my final exams, I was offered my first paying job as a doctor: as an intern, working under supervision, at Royal Hobart Hospital.

My first term at the hospital was in emergency medicine, which I loved. It could be frantic on Friday and Saturday nights, with lots of patients and not enough staff. The hospital was always squeezed for beds on those nights. I soon realised that to get new patients admitted, I needed to convince the admitting doctor that they were seriously ill.

My first patient with a heart attack was an experience. He had classic symptoms: central chest pain radiating down his left arm and up to his jaw, with an ECG showing what's called ST elevation. I called the senior resident to run through the symptoms so she could decide whether to admit him. My inexperience showed when I took what must have been fifteen minutes to detail everything I could think of about the patient. I later realised that all I'd needed to do was describe the chest pain and the ECG result.

After my time in emergency, I also had terms at the hospital in internal medicine, surgery, anaesthetics, emergency again, and a night shift covering both emergency and wards.

Towards the end of my intern year, I met Anita Mudge, who was a physiotherapist at the hospital. She came from Queensland and really appreciated the Tassie outdoors. I thought she was an amazingly warm, kind and fun person and we got on brilliantly. We quickly fell in love.

As the year finished, I essentially had three options for the next stage of my career. Did I want to train to be a GP, a surgeon or a physician, specialising in a field of internal medicine such as cardiology, neurology or gastroenterology? I favoured becoming a physician but that meant committing to three more years' training in Tassie.

I really liked the practical side of medicine. I enjoyed making a difference for patients quickly. Now, aged almost 25, I realised I was ambitious. I wanted to become a specialist and I wanted to see more of the world. It was time to leave.

5

NEW WORLDS

I weighed up the options for leaving Tasmania with a friend from medical school, Louise Owen, who was also finishing as an intern at Royal Hobart Hospital. We decided to apply to be resident medical officers at Royal Adelaide Hospital and were both delighted to be accepted.

It was a new part of Australia to discover and a step towards seeing more of the world. I didn't want to spend my life just in Tassie, though I planned to settle there later in my career. I was convinced it was the best place in the world to live and I had so many friends there. But I was keen to do a lot more travelling first.

Anita and I wanted to continue our new relationship, so we agreed to visit each other when we could.

Adelaide was . . . not what I expected. While bigger than Hobart, I liked that it was nowhere near as bustling and traffic-filled as Melbourne and Sydney. But I found it challenging at first making new friends and working in a different hospital system.

When I started at Royal Adelaide, I was grateful that, in Hobart, I'd learned practical medical skills, taken on responsibility and developed confidence treating patients. I'd delivered many babies and cared for new mothers afterwards. I'd put in many central lines (intravenous lines that go up to near the heart), where there's a lot of what surgeons call 'tiger country' around major blood vessels; you can kill a patient if you don't know what you're doing. I'd intubated patients (inserting a tube to keep their windpipe open). I felt I'd had more opportunities to learn these procedures— under supervision and respecting the risks—than some of the junior Adelaide doctors.

My first term was in the emergency department, which, at the time, didn't have registrars to supervise junior residents like me, or a registrar-training scheme. I was sometimes the most experienced doctor in the department, including on busy night shifts. It was a lot of responsibility so early on but I didn't feel out of my depth. I thought I handled the pressure well.

There was a powerful moment late one Saturday night when a patient who seemed drunk and confused came into emergency. It would have been easy to put his condition down to too much alcohol except that an intern and I noticed that one of his pupils was more dilated than the other, which might have been an indication of bleeding in the cranium. We sent him for tests, which confirmed this was in fact what was happening, and he received the treatment he needed. But if we'd missed that sign, the patient could easily have died.

The lesson: don't assume alcohol is the cause of everything that brings a patient to an emergency department on a Saturday night.

I had other stints at Royal Adelaide—in psychiatry, internal medicine, emergency again and rehabilitation, which took me to a rehab hospital to work with patients who'd had strokes and spinal injuries. One day I hopped in a wheelchair to play basketball with spinal patients and amputees. Most of the time as a junior doctor you're working so hard that you don't get to have light-hearted experiences like this. The patients were much more skilful than me and they laughed freely when I made mistakes. I admired their spirit after having had their lives turned upside down.

Louise's doctor friends were going overseas so we rented their house in leafy Norwood. I started playing footy for a club called St Peter's Old Collegians. It wasn't as enjoyable as I'd been hoping, partly because I was working long hours at the hospital, and wasn't in peak form as a result, and also because the social side of football in Adelaide was very different to how it had been in Hobart.

Whenever I'd felt like going out in Tassie, there were three pubs where I'd know dozens of people a short walk away. My friends and I never arranged to meet other friends;

they were just there wherever I went. If I visited Salamanca Market on a Saturday morning, I'd know lots of people having breakfast or shopping at the stalls. It was different in Adelaide. The guys who grew up there had established networks of friends. That meant I felt like an outsider at times, which was a jolt.

People were nice to me . . . but I started to wish I was still in Tassie.

Around this time, a terrific pathology trainee at the hospital, Bastiaan de Boer, advised me that 'Pathology is fantastic. You should give it a go.' I hadn't forgotten how inspired I'd been by the pathologists who had taught me at university, so I looked into how the training system worked and the commitment and sacrifices I'd need to make to become a pathologist. I could see making a diagnosis was an intellectual challenge. A pathologist had to weigh up a lot of information—assessing what are called pathological features—to come up with the right diagnosis and to help a patient get the best treatment. I wondered whether it could be a career for me.

———

I looked forward to whenever Anita and I could see each other. Once I surprised her at Adelaide airport by arriving with her luggage on the baggage carousel while wearing a Pink Panther outfit, which she thought was funny. We were getting on really well, even if we were only able to see each other once a month. When she came to South Australia, we visited the Barossa Valley and McLaren Vale, staying in bed and breakfasts and checking out wineries and restaurants. We camped in the Flinders Ranges and went for walks.

It was an altogether darker experience when I visited Anita in Tasmania another weekend. We were driving from Launceston to Hobart late one Sunday night when we came across a car crash—a head-on collision—on the Midland Highway just outside Oatlands. I got out of the car and started doing whatever I could to help.

People were lying badly injured on the road; some were dead and others had broken limbs. When an ambulance arrived, I used their equipment to intubate two people on the roadside. One was too severely injured and didn't make it.

Four people died.

Everyone in the accident was about our age. I didn't know any of them, which was surprising given it was the highway from Hobart to Launceston. But people I knew did know them. The two carloads of people had been heading home in opposite directions after being away for the weekend. Like Anita and me, they were probably quietly enjoying the drive until the horror of the collision.

I was offered grief counselling afterwards from Hobart. I said I was fine and was back in Adelaide anyway. I was more worried about how Anita was coping but it was definitely traumatic for both of us. The accident scene was worse than anything I'd seen in emergency departments or while joining ambulance crews as a medical student. Looking back, I still don't think I needed that counselling but the accident remains a vivid memory.

Back at work, near the end of our one-year terms, Louise left for Melbourne, where her boyfriend Owen, also a doctor, had gone for advanced training in nuclear medicine. I still didn't have a strong network of friends in Adelaide so I decided to look for another job somewhere else.

A colleague told me how much he'd enjoyed working at Gosford District Hospital (now Gosford Hospital) on the NSW Central Coast. I applied and was accepted there as a senior resident medical officer (the 'senior' meant I was in my second year as a resident).

Anita decided to join me in Gosford. After she quit her job in Hobart, she and I drove from Adelaide to Brisbane to visit her parents for Christmas. She landed a job at the same hospital and we moved into an amazing house on Avoca Beach with a medical-school friend, Duncan Guy, and his partner, Kathy Cristofani, another doctor. I surfed and played footy for a local team, the Terrigal Panthers.

We were in such a sensational spot that people would ring me first thing in the morning for a surf report. Anita and I often cycled into work and I raced my first triathlon. I figured I'd be well suited as I'd done fun runs since I was a kid, I liked swimming and I was commuting on my bike. While my result was nothing special, I loved racing—the exercise, the competition and the company of a lot of other active people.

The Central Coast was a friendly place and the doctors at the hospital were a relaxed bunch. Everyone working there seemed to be an outsider to the area and, like me, they loved the lifestyle. I felt I fitted in better there than in Adelaide.

It was a brilliant year but, when my term was up, Anita and I decided we wanted to see more of the world, especially Europe. We also thought it would be good to get experience in medicine in another country, so we planned a trip to Scandinavia. Anita's mum had grown up in Denmark, and she had relatives in Copenhagen and Jutland we could visit. It seemed like a stunning part of the world.

To save money for the trip, I worked for three months as a locum GP at a medical centre in Gosford and found it really rewarding helping patients. One man was incredibly grateful when I diagnosed him with melanoma and he was able to get treatment. I saw at times like that how being a GP could be really satisfying.

Then it was time to head to Europe. As well as seeing new places, Anita and I were excited about immersing ourselves in different cultures. Arriving in Denmark, which seemed so beautiful and stylish, we stayed with Anita's aunt then set off travelling around Scandinavia, mostly on trains and camping. There was one big difference from camping in Tassie: it was June so even if we arrived somewhere at midnight, it was always light, which made it easy to set up our tent.

We went to Norway, where camping was free, and visited Stavanger, Oslo, Bergen, Trondheim and the Lofoten Islands, then travelled through the north of Sweden and Finland and back south to Helsinki and Stockholm. The fresh air, stunning scenery, rich history and Scandinavian culture were intoxicating, like nothing I'd ever experienced.

Anita and I enjoyed travelling together, but then, inevitably, we started to run out of money. We decided to head to England and get jobs.

Anita found us a one-room place in South Kensington in London, and landed a job as a physio in a hospital. I took on a month's work as a senior house officer in cardiology at Royal Papworth Hospital, on the outskirts of Cambridge. While it was the national heart and lung transplant centre, it seemed to be located in the middle of nowhere.

It was a curious place for an Australian to work, with one of my bosses grandly called 'Sir Professor'. I tested patients' hearts under exercise, and helped with angiograms that checked for blood-vessel abnormalities and blockages. I also removed catheters when patients returned to their wards, which meant I had the humbling job of keeping pressure on each patient's groin for twenty minutes to stop any bleeding.

I worked for another month as a medical registrar at a hospital in north London that I'd better keep nameless. In Australia, my experience was that the consultant in charge of a registrar at a hospital would normally come in at the end of the consultant's period on call to help formulate treatment plans for patients. At this hospital, I didn't even meet some of these consultants. During my time, they didn't visit the hospital on ward rounds even when they were on call, which was different to standard practice in Australia. I managed well enough without them but was surprised by the system.

I then took a short-term locum job at University College Hospital in London. As a locum at these English hospitals, I was paid for every hour I worked, so the money was crazily good, which helped with the cost of living in England. I was getting to experience a different health system, and Anita and I could afford to keep travelling when the time was right.

During all these short-term jobs, what I wanted to do for a career kept changing. While the outstanding teachers I'd had in Tassie meant I'd enjoyed pathology at medical school, I wondered how much I'd enjoy spending my career in a laboratory.

For a while, I considered becoming an emergency medicine specialist—fixing patients in crisis. I'd learned that I dealt well with pressure and loved the adrenaline of the job. But as I spent more time in emergency departments, I recognised that there was a downside to always doing shift work, and there was less follow-through with patients. I would usually only see them once. Either they were fixed up, admitted to hospital to be looked after by other teams, or sent home. My connection with them was often a one-off.

Neurology was another career I thought about. I loved figuring out the cause of a patient's neurological problem. You had to really use your intellect and consider many factors to work out the right diagnosis. But, once a condition was diagnosed, there were often only limited treatments available back then.

There were also times I considered becoming a cardiologist or a gastroenterologist. I really liked doing physical procedures that fixed patients. And when I was working with children in Gosford, I felt like paediatrics would be a satisfying career. What appealed was that most of the time kids recovered when you diagnosed and treated them. That was as gratifying as it was heartwarming.

Often, I'd found the specialty I was most interested in depended not so much on the patients' medical problems but on the bosses I was working with. If I liked them, I could see myself working in that field. If I didn't, well, there were plenty of other challenging and rewarding roles in medicine.

I always tried to get the most from every job I did. Looking back, I can see that the desire to keep learning from everyone I worked with—doctors, nurses, other health professionals—and take lessons from every mistake I made was valuable preparation for my career. Thankfully, none of those mistakes were life-threatening or seriously affected patients.

I'd heard from a Tassie friend that Royal Hobart Hospital was advertising for a first-year trainee registrar (the next step up from resident, in a formal training scheme) in pathology. After talking it over with Anita, who knew I wanted to live in Tassie again, I mailed off an application but missed out. I was disappointed. Understandably, the job went to someone talented who was already working there.

But before leaving for Europe, I'd mentioned to my Uncle Tony, a paediatrician in Canberra, that I'd been thinking about pathology as a career after Bastiaan de Boer's recommendation. Out of the blue, Tony sent me an application form for a trainee registrar position in anatomical pathology at Canberra Hospital. It would be a path to becoming a pathologist, with a minimum of five years' training, multiple exams, working and learning under supervision during the day, and studying at night and on weekends.

Pathologists can specialise in the likes of haematology (diagnosing such blood-related illnesses as anaemia, leukemia and lymphoma); immunopathology (diagnosing diseases that affect the immune system); genetic pathology (analysing genomic data); forensic pathology (identifying the cause and circumstances of death); microbiology (diagnosing diseases caused by infection); and clinical chemistry (analysing abnormalities in blood). But I would be specialising in anatomical pathology, diagnosing cancer and other diseases from tissue samples.

Thinking through the Canberra job, I doubted the team there would hire someone they didn't know. And when Anita and I talked it over, we weren't sure we wanted to go back to Australia yet. But it was a rare opportunity and Royal Hobart was out of the question now. If I did get the job, Canberra would be another adventure.

I applied, not expecting to be successful, and was surprised when they wrote back and offered me a position. I didn't realise until later that they were offering the job of a haematology registrar at the hospital—a different position—and I'd be analysing blood rather than tissue.

Weighing up the pros and cons, Anita and I thought it sounded promising. Canberra had always seemed like a terrific place to visit. She said she'd be happy working as a general physio there. We knew some people in the national capital, too. I got on well with my Uncle Tony and his family, and there was also the cousin I had first met in South Africa, Chris, and his girlfriend Isobelle, who were both pharmacists at the hospital. And neither Anita nor I were looking forward to the bitter cold of a grey English winter.

We decided to head home. I accepted the job.

––––––

It turned out to be a fantastic move. As a haematology registrar, most of my time would normally be spent either performing and interpreting bone-marrow biopsies or analysing blood results in the laboratory. But, to help one of the consultants, I was asked to see patients with diseases like lymphoma and leukaemia at a weekly clinic. Having been used to seeing patients in any number of roles since medical school, I enjoyed this part of my role. It was clear that haematology was a better option at this stage of my career.

If I'd got the job I initially applied for, as an anatomical pathology registrar, I would have been a junior member of a team and much of my work would have been cutting up specimens and writing reports. I wouldn't have had the same responsibility I'd had when I worked in emergency departments, on UK hospital wards and as a locum GP. And I wouldn't have been spending any time with patients, either. In retrospect, I wonder whether I would have stuck with anatomical pathology had I got the original job; whether

I would have missed having contact with patients too much if it happened too abruptly.

When someone left and I had the chance to switch to anatomical pathology after two weeks, I decided to stick with haematology for a year. My pathology training would take longer but the experience would be invaluable.

The more I immersed myself in pathology, the more rewarding I found it. I loved the science behind it and the intellectual challenge. Diagnosing patients was a lot more involved than just saying whether their condition was benign or malignant. For cancer patients, the pathological features were often major factors in determining not only the most likely outcome for the patient but also the most appropriate treatment.

By this time in my life, I'd realised how driven I was— and not just about building a successful career. I wanted to give patients the right diagnosis—and also identify these key pathological features that help determine their likely outcome—so they could be treated and return to being healthy again. I wanted to carry out research to improve our understanding of diseases, what caused them and how they could be managed as well as possible. I wanted to know more about the science behind what pathologists did and see if I could improve it.

After getting through my haematology exams at the end of the year, I decided it was the right time to transfer to anatomical pathology. True, it lacked so much direct contact with patients. But I could see that to do it well, I'd need to know about the whole body and every disease—more than I needed to know in haematology. Diagnosis was a fascinating exercise in knowledge and skill. And I'd get to work with really smart people, trying to sort out patients' problems, every day. I liked all of that.

ACT Pathology, where I was working, was an excellent place to train. The professor in charge, Peter Herdson, was an affable New Zealander who hosted a lunch for the trainees and a Friday-night party for the whole pathology department every three months. It was an important lesson for my later work in medicine: Peter valued everyone, saw the benefits of sharing knowledge, encouraged up-and-comers, and made pathologists and laboratory staff feel part of a team. There was no medical school in Canberra at the time, so all the doctors had trained elsewhere and they were all looking to form new social networks, which made it an easy place to make friends.

As part of our training, a different pathology registrar delivered a talk every week. It was impressive how many specialists and other staff from the department attended. That desire to keep learning throughout your career was another lesson for later life.

I was also gaining experience by writing up some of my most interesting cases to submit as articles to *Pathology*, the journal of the Royal College of Pathologists of Australasia.

My first paper was on an unusual case, where I'd had to determine the cause of a patient's mysterious death in hospital. In an autopsy, I found he had a high eosinophil (white blood cell) level and vasculitis (inflammation in the blood-vessel walls) in his lungs and elsewhere. He had died from a rare disorder called Churg–Strauss Syndrome, which caused inflammation that restricted blood flow to organs and tissues.

My first ever paper was published! It turned out to be the only one in my career on which I was the sole author. I quickly realised that, when writing a paper, it was best to have input from other people in the department to make it as strong as possible—another lesson about the benefits of collaboration and teamwork. I was pleased when Peter Herdson asked me to collaborate with him on a report called 'Defining moments in medicine—Pathology' for *The Medical Journal of Australia*.

It felt like it was all coming together in Canberra. I liked the department and the people; I was getting positive feedback from my bosses; Anita was working as a physio at Canberra Hospital; and we were really enjoying each other's company and the lifestyle we had in the national capital. We were living in a townhouse in Yarralumla, so I was running around the lake and often cycling to work to keep fit. I raced some more triathlons and Anita joined in, too. We tried hard but there were many better competitors in our age groups.

On weekends, we'd go walking in Kosciuszko National Park, out the back of the Blue Mountains, Warrumbungle National Park and on the NSW south coast. In winter, we went skiing at Thredbo and Perisher.

ACT Pathology was a small unit, so my work was closely watched. If I got something right, there was a pat on the back. If I did something wrong, the senior pathologists were on to me to fix it up and teach me what I should have done. I kept learning.

There were inspiring people to look up to as role models, too. One of my fellow anatomical pathology trainees was Jane Dahlstrom, who was super smart, hardworking, extremely motivated and had six children. Seeing how committed Jane was inspired me to push myself both at work and while studying at night and on weekends. It was no surprise that she later became inaugural dean of the Australian National University's new College of Health & Medicine in Canberra.

On Wednesday afternoons, I'd often drive to Sydney for training sessions called 'too hards' at the University of Sydney, with a lecture afterwards at RPA. Pathology registrars brought along their tricky cases, everyone studied the slides, and there were discussions about what each slide showed and what the diagnosis was. It was always stimulating; there was a lot to think about on the three-hour drive back the same night.

Going to these 'too hards' sessions, it struck me, by what I was able to contribute, how much I'd learned in Canberra. I'd gained a huge amount from the variety in my career so far. I knew that if I was going to enjoy being an anatomical pathologist, I would have to be good at it.

———

To take the next step up from being a registrar—becoming a specialist—I needed to pass the Royal College of Pathologists' two-part exam in anatomical pathology. I studied hard and got through the Part I exams in 1998.

Because there was a requirement that anyone taking these exams had to have worked in at least two institutions, I had to leave Canberra after almost four years—one year as a haematology registrar and nearly three years as an anatomical pathology registrar. While I still wanted to go back to Tassie at some stage, I thought either RPA in Sydney or, as a backup, the pathology lab PathWest in Perth would be the best places to finish my training.

I applied to join both and was accepted at both. Anita and I thought Sydney had a lot going for it—we knew people there, it would be an exciting place to live and there would be plenty of work opportunities for her.

We decided on the RPA job and moved to Sydney. We rented a place near the hospital and moved all our furniture from Canberra, and Anita found a job at Sydney Children's Hospital at Randwick.

I didn't love everything about Sydney. I went for my one and only surf at Bondi with a friend from Tassie in the first week. My friend dropped in on another surfer whose mates wanted to rough us up in the car park afterwards. I thought, 'I've got better things to do with my time'—and knew I'd be too busy to surf much, anyway. I had to pass the Part II exam and get my career as a pathologist rolling.

I met some outstanding people at RPA. Stan McCarthy, the consultant in pathology at the hospital, was recognised as the country's top pathologist. Every year, he was sent thousands of cases that pathologists all over Australia and around the world were having trouble diagnosing. I was blown away by his skill in recognising melanoma and other tumours, and by how he always had time to help anyone who needed it.

A warm and softly spoken man who had just turned 60, Stan was a brilliant teacher. When he shared some of these challenging cases to help me learn, he seemed to genuinely value my opinion. Trying to diagnose them was a stimulating challenge. When I very occasionally came up with a diagnosis he hadn't thought of, he was delighted and I felt proud.

But Stan helped everyone. If a registrar or specialist pathologist wanted advice, he immediately stopped what he was doing, rather than saying, 'Leave it with me and I'll get back to you.' If you looked down the microscope with Stan, he would teach you rather than just giving his opinion. I found his expertise, generosity and willingness to help others inspirational. I've tried to emulate it in my own career.

While most consultants interacted regularly with trainees, Stan went further. He came along to a touch footy game that the registrars and our friends played on Sunday afternoons, first at Centennial Park and then at Camperdown Oval. It was a fun social game that both Anita and I played. Stan brought along his wife Valerie and tiny daughter Rose-Lynn, who later became a pathology registrar at RPA. As someone who loved rugby union among other sports and had stayed fit, he was a skilful player who could beat defenders with a goosestep. But Stan was far from being a show-off: reflecting his generous nature, he regularly passed the ball to players who hadn't been involved much in the game so they could score.

Stan became a mentor and fantastic friend. We would have lunch in the tea room of the anatomical pathology department just about every day. He always brought the same thing . . . a tin of tuna that he spread on bread, sometimes with tomato and lettuce, and a piece of fruit. His wise words included advising me never to diagnose a challenging case after 3 p.m.: a pathologist needed to be fresh and alert for tricky cases.

While I didn't get to know her much until later, one of the other pathology registrars who joined these touch footy games was Katie Nicoll. She seemed warm and friendly and, years later, would have a bigger influence on my life than anyone else.

Dr Kerry Crotty, who taught at the University of Sydney, was another one of the brilliant people I met at RPA. She struck me as someone who always spoke up for what she believed was the right thing. Like Stan, she was constantly putting in extra time and effort.

Professor Peter Russell, whose expertise was in gynaecological pathology, was another senior figure at RPA who made time to help registrars. A man who loved his family, restaurants, wine and good holidays, he was an excellent advocate for the department with the hospital administration.

Paul 'Tex' McKenzie, who was the acting head of the department when Peter went on holidays, was a warm, sensible, highly intelligent and modest pathologist with an excellent sense of humour. Tex and his wife Margaret, a GP, had bought a dilapidated mansion, Abbotsford House, in the inner west suburb of Abbotsford, to renovate into a grand residence. In his retirement, Paul became an accomplished artist who painted my portrait for the Archibald Prize. It wasn't a finalist but I admired the skill he brought to the portrait.

I was also impressed when I met one of the best-known doctors at the hospital, Professor Chris O'Brien, who was the face of the hit TV show *RPA*. A professor of surgery at the University of Sydney and director of the Sydney Head and Neck Cancer Institute, he was friendly and eloquent. I liked that he seemed to value everyone from medical students to other consultants, no matter where they were in the medical hierarchy.

Like Stan, Chris was a generation older than me but was warm, friendly and charismatic. When we hit it off, he included me in discussions and asked questions that made me feel like he valued what I said. After one of our regular multidisciplinary team meetings, Chris recommended I do more work overseas, which was what he'd done, and offered to organise a fellowship in the US. While I didn't take up the offer—other opportunities came up when I finished my training—he was generous to make it.

All in all, I was learning a huge amount as a pathologist, especially about bone and soft-tissue tumours, studying hard for my Part II exams and being inspired by exceptional people at RPA.

As a registrar, I'd regularly attend multidisciplinary team meetings, in which experts from various fields discussed the diagnoses of their patients and how they should be treated. I enjoyed contributing a pathologist's perspective to these discussions.

And I kept writing papers for journals. The articles I published from my years in Canberra and early time in Sydney—there was always a lag between writing and publication—covered a range of fascinating cases. They might not mean much outside the medical community but they included a fine-needle biopsy diagnosis of a hepatocellular carcinoma (liver cancer) that had metastasised to the orbit (skull); a patient with middle lobe syndrome in a lung from a solitary bronchial papilloma; an inverted duct tumour of the minor salivary gland; and a patient with acute basophilic leukaemia, a rare type of blood disorder that didn't show up in blood tests but was detectable in liver-function tests. I was especially proud of a paper setting out previously undescribed features of a soft-tissue cancer that had just been defined: hyalinising spindle cell tumour with giant rosettes, later recognised as a subtype of another rare soft-tissue tumour called low grade fibromyxoid sarcoma.

Papers like these pushed forward the understanding of unusual cancers that other specialists might not have encountered. They meant sacrificing some spare time, though. I had to type up these papers in triplicate. My photos of slides took three weeks to be processed, then had to be repeated if they were out of focus. I used Letraset, a now long-outdated form of dry-transfer lettering, to add captions.

While publishing these papers helped my career, my motivation was trying to make a difference. When you make a diagnosis for one patient, you help that patient. When you do research, you can help many patients. If we keep improving our knowledge of diseases, we can improve diagnosis, management and ultimately outcomes for patients.

———————

Everything was going well until I sat for my Part II exams in 1999. I got a call later from Dr David Nevell, the state councillor for the Royal College of Pathologists, who told me I'd failed.

I'd known it wouldn't be easy: these exams are notoriously difficult. But it was the first time I'd ever failed an exam. I was devastated. I had to go into work with all these people I admired—all these friends—who knew I'd failed. I was embarrassed. Humiliated.

Stan was shocked but encouraged me to keep working towards passing when I was eligible to sit the exam again in a year. Kerry Crotty and Paul McKenzie reassured me I would get through next time.

While everyone in the pathology department was kind, I was down for a couple of weeks. Not exactly kicking stones, but probably not much fun to be around.

One strength I had, though, was to be strategic in a crisis. It had helped when I'd just scraped through my second-year university exams. This time I realised I'd misinterpreted a couple of slides in the diagnosis exam because I hadn't seen enough cases yet to recognise subtle differences. But I knew I'd get another year of experience diagnosing slides before I could sit for Part II again, so I decided to focus on exam technique instead.

Generous friends and colleagues set practice exams that I did every weekend. Especially helpful was Fiona Bonar, an Irish pathologist from private lab Douglass Hanly Moir, who was a star in bone and soft-tissue tumours.

Going into the exam, I told myself that there was no way I was going to fail again. But I was still anxious. The answers were never clear-cut because it wasn't possible to diagnose some cases on the information given. That meant you had to present a plan for how you'd arrive at the right diagnosis, including the tests you'd use to narrow down the possibilities.

In August 2000, I resat the Part II exam and felt like I'd nailed it this time. There was no ominous phone call breaking bad news. When the results came out, I was overjoyed—and more than a little relieved—to have passed.

Fifteen years after I had started at medical school, my career as a pathologist could now get underway.

6

SPECIALISING IN MELANOMA

The timing was perfect to enjoy the 2000 Olympics in Sydney before looking for a job. Anita and I had plenty of tickets thanks to an impetuous decision I'd made with a friend, St Vincent's Hospital pathologist Wade Barrett. We'd requested a bunch of tickets in the ballot, testing the limits of our credit cards, expecting we'd only get some of them. We ended up getting everything, but it was worth every cent.

Anita and I thoroughly enjoyed watching gymnastics, hockey, the marathon, athletics and Cathy Freeman's incredible win in the 400 metres in the main stadium. It was the most fantastically upbeat time in Sydney. Everyone was friendly, it was sunny and public transport ran smoothly. As we headed home from the stadium late at night, cheerful passengers sang. I was already feeling good after passing my exams but the atmosphere at the Games made it an even more special time.

We were loving our move to Sydney.

At work, I had decided what I wanted to be: a pathologist at RPA, or at another major teaching hospital, where the cases I'd be working with would be complex and fascinating. I thought that helping patients by diagnosing and reporting these cases accurately would be both rewarding and a valuable community contribution. One trouble, though, was that RPA's pathology department was small, with the equivalent of only seven full-time jobs. But a pathologist who had worked at the hospital for a remarkable 46 years, Dr Tatiana Jelihovsky, was retiring, so there was a half-time job going. I applied.

I was delighted to get it, becoming a half-time specialist in anatomical pathology. This meant I would be diagnosing challenging cases across every specialty, including lung, gastrointestinal and gynaecological diseases, and sometimes brain tumours.

Around the same time, at the instigation of Kerry Crotty, the Melanoma and Skin Cancer Research Institute (MASCRI), which was part of the Sydney Melanoma Unit, advertised a pathology research fellowship.

Patients who had been referred to the Unit were often sent by a GP or a surgeon who worked elsewhere, with a diagnosis made by an 'outside' pathologist. Given that it was difficult to distinguish a melanoma from a benign mole in about 20 per cent of cases, the unit's surgeons wanted these biopsy results reviewed to confirm patients had melanoma before starting treatment. These reviews were also an opportunity to collect more detailed pathological data, which would refine our understanding of the seriousness of the case and indicate the best treatment.

The unit also wanted extra data for research. It would be invaluable to know such factors as the thickness of the tumour, whether it was ulcerated, the mitotic rate (the speed at which cancer cells divide and grow), whether there was cancer in the lymphatic system or blood vessels, and, if the tumour had been excised for a biopsy, how close it was to the edges of the cut.

Because the pathology department didn't have enough staff to carry out all this work, MASCRI was seeking a pathology research fellow. I was already passionate about research so I applied.

The decision on awarding the fellowship was down to a five-person panel that included two highly regarded surgeons: Professor Bill McCarthy—no relation to Stan—who was the head of MASCRI, and Professor John Thompson, who was executive director of the Sydney Melanoma Unit. Knowing I already had a half-time job, they offered me the fellowship as a half-time position. I gratefully accepted.

It definitely didn't feel like it at the time but failing the Part II exam the year before had been a blessing. It drove me to work harder to become a better pathologist, it meant that the decision-makers at the hospital knew me better, and the timing was perfect—two golden opportunities had come up just as I finished my training.

I threw myself into the work.

While I was interested in bone and soft-tissue tumours, they were relatively rare. Melanoma was much more common, which made it an appealing specialisation. It meant I could help many more patients—a natural instinct that my mentor Stan McCarthy and John Thompson encouraged. And RPA, I figured, was the perfect place to focus on it.

The hospital had patients referred from around the country and overseas, many with tumours that were difficult to diagnose. Getting an accurate diagnosis—and detailed assessment of features that determined prognosis and treatment—was essential and I relished the challenge.

People think of pathology as being definitive: looking down the microscope, you determine whether something is cancerous or benign. But it's much more subjective than that. Pathologists have to interpret a slide, and this interpretation is based on their knowledge, experience and the range of tests they do. If the diagnosis isn't clear-cut, they make what's called a differential diagnosis—the most likely diagnosis, followed by other possibilities in descending order. My approach was to study a tissue sample, then come up with a differential diagnosis *before* reading the clinical notes, so I didn't jump to any conclusions. That was something Stan taught me.

A skin tissue sample can reveal quite a bit about patients. It can show if they've had a lot of sun exposure. From the pathological features, you can usually tell whether the sample is from a patient's arm, back, face or wherever. Certain features show if a patient is older, or, if they're a woman, whether she could be pregnant. If I needed more information to make a definite diagnosis, I would ring the referring doctor and ask about the lesion in question: had it developed recently, had it changed, were there any other relevant factors? If the lesion was recent or had changed appearance, it was more likely to be melanoma. If a patient was older— say, 70—there was a higher risk that what appeared to be a benign mole could be melanoma.

The pathologist's diagnosis is absolutely crucial in determining how a patient is going to be treated. The assessment of a whole range of pathological features that help determine their prognosis and, in some cases, likely response to drug treatments, is also very important. All of this information has to be accurate. If it isn't, patients might not get the treatment they need to save their life.

Australia has the world's highest rate of skin cancer— a result of sun exposure from our outdoor lifestyle, the fair skin of people with European heritage and the relatively high levels of UV radiation here. For me, specialising in melanoma made sense. It provided opportunities to undertake research that would improve outcomes for a huge number of patients.

———

A little history . . .

Throughout the first half of the twentieth century, there was a powerful narrative that Australia was a sun-loving culture, and that having a tan was a healthy look. My friends and I were thinking this way when we applied baby oil at the beach. It took decades to realise the deadly consequences as more people were diagnosed with—and died from—melanoma.

In 1957, a landmark paper by Dr Henry Oliver Lancaster and Dr Janet Nelson, published in *The Medical Journal of Australia*, showed sunlight exposure was likely the main cause of melanoma and that there was a direct link between the death rate from the disease and the distance people lived from the equator. They found the country's highest melanoma rates were in Queensland, with progressively lower rates in New South Wales, then Victoria and Tasmania.

In the early 1960s, Swiss chemist Franz Greiter, who had invented the first modern sunscreen after being badly sunburnt climbing Mount Piz Buin, developed the sun protection factor (SPF) rating. Around the same time, Australian surgeon Dr Gerry Milton recognised how high the rates of melanoma were in this country compared to the rest of the world. So, with fellow surgeon Bill McCarthy, he set up the Sydney Melanoma Clinic at Sydney Hospital in 1965. As patient numbers swelled, they began clinical trials that included evaluating the optimal extent of surgery, immune-related therapies and chemotherapy and, because advanced melanoma was effectively terminal, provided palliative care.

In the early 1980s, the clinic moved to RPA, which allowed it to become a clinical unit within the University of Sydney, and changed its name to the Sydney Melanoma Unit.

Bill McCarthy championed the famous 'slip, slop, slap' campaign on behalf of the Unit and the New South Wales Cancer Council—TV commercials urging Australians to slip on a shirt, slop on sunblock and slap on a sunhat when out in the sun—that drew attention to the risks of sun exposure.

When I started my half-time fellowship, John Thompson, the intellectually-minded surgeon who ran the Unit, saw it as a chance to ramp up research. At the time, John was one of an elite group of surgeons who knew how to conduct and write up research that could affect the management of large numbers of patients, most of whom they would never see. While many surgeons—and indeed doctors—only focused on their own patients, John recognised that research could improve the treatment of many more. So, from day one, he became a second mentor, encouraging me and supporting me to undertake research and write up papers for publication.

While they were very different people, John and Stan had a lot in common. They were humble, hardworking and dedicated; they encouraged other people, especially younger colleagues, and valued the expertise of others; they cared deeply about their patients; and they were driven more by helping people than by financial rewards.

They represented the kind of doctor I wanted to be. I admired their values and I shared them.

One of the first tasks in my fellowship was collecting melanoma tissue and blood samples to build a biospecimen bank. It would supplement the unit's extensive database of melanoma patient details and become a powerful tool for research.

A month after I started work as a 50 per cent staff special-ist and 50 per cent research fellow, the World Melanoma Congress was held in Venice. As an international authority, Stan was delivering a talk and encouraged me to come along with him. It was a chance to see the latest developments in treatment and research.

For a newcomer to the field, the conference in snowy, magical, historic Venice was an exhilarating experience. Stan was such a generous mentor that he introduced me to the world leaders in melanoma, including renowned pathol-ogists Professor Alistair Cochran from the University of California, Los Angeles (UCLA) and Professor Marty Mihm from Harvard. I helped Stan prepare his talk on subungual melanoma (a rare disease of the toenails or fingernails) and took in everything I could.

I was ambitious to learn and make my own name. Back at RPA, I had follow-up emails from people I'd met at the conference who were interested in our work. The more we formed relationships with international melanoma experts, the more collaborative research we could do on the most urgent issues. It was a valuable trip.

One night in September 2001, Anita and I bought a house at an auction in the inner west suburb of Newtown. We'd been looking for a while and finally took the plunge. The next morning we woke up, turned on the TV and saw the Twin Towers falling in New York.

It was a turbulent time everywhere, including in my life. The pressure of committing to a mortgage brought up ques-tions for Anita and me about where we were heading in our lives. After an amazing ten years of shared experiences, we made the painful decision to break up. It was shattering. Our relationship—where we'd been, the adventures we'd had, her sacrifices while I was studying for the pathology exams—had been a major part of my growing up in my late twenties and early thirties.

Anita moved to Coogee, closer to her work at Sydney Children's Hospital in Randwick. To get through a rough time, I doubled down on work.

Still extremely keen to learn more about pathology and gain more experience, I continued going to and was now teaching at the 'too hards' sessions that I used to drive up from Canberra to attend. When Kerry Crotty and Paul McKenzie needed a new coordinator, I put up my hand. I added Saturday sessions as part of a program called Recent Advances in Pathology. They were practical classes that featured slides on particular topics. The program was a hit and eventually turned into what was called the RPA Diagnostic Surgical Pathology Course, held over a week every year.

I also volunteered for roles with other professional organisations, including the editorial board of the journal *Pathology*, an anatomical pathology education subcommittee of the Royal College of Pathologists, a Central Sydney Area Health Service quality assurance committee, and a taskforce on bone and soft-tissue tumour services. It was extra work but it seemed like it was valuable.

One Sunday, Stan took me down to an annual social cricket game and barbecue, hosted by Bill McCarthy at his farm near Nowra, for everyone associated with MASCRI and the Sydney Melanoma Unit. It was dawning on me how important teams were in medicine. Bill, who saw this day as a fun team-building exercise, knew that groups of people with complementary skills could make a bigger difference for patients and for research than individuals working on their own. Bill also recognised early that it was important to prevent skin cancer as well as treat it, and he had been a strong force in sourcing philanthropic and government funding for research.

Led by John Thompson in Australia, one of the big advances in melanoma treatment had been what was called a sentinel node biopsy, a procedure in which a surgeon removed both a primary tumour and any lymph nodes directly draining from it to see if they contained cancer cells. If there were no cancer cells, it meant the melanoma hadn't spread to other lymph nodes and was also less likely to have reached other parts of the body. It was at a sentinel node conference in Yokohama, Japan, that I experienced another significant moment in my career.

During a session, I politely took issue with Dr Don Morton, the surgeon who had developed the sentinel node biopsy with Alistair Cochran at UCLA. He said in his presentation that injecting carbon dye into the primary melanoma site to see whether it was detectable in lymph nodes would make less work for pathologists, which wasn't accurate. I pointed out that pathologists would still need to study all sections of the tumour. While I could have been seen as an upstart correcting one of the gurus of the field, my comments seemed to get the respect of the international experts at the meeting and drew attention to the importance of the work we were doing in Sydney.

When I later delivered two talks on different aspects of the sentinel node research that we had done at the Unit, Don Morton and Alistair Cochran came along and asked questions. It felt like what I was learning at RPA had value even for melanoma leaders overseas.

––––––––

It was around this time that I got to know Katie Nicoll, who I'd first met when we were both pathology registrars at RPA and played weekend touch footy games. She was engaging and interesting to talk to—confident, intelligent, adventurous, worldly and down to earth, with an excellent sense of humour. When I saw her going out of her way to help people—even those she'd just met—I could see how generous she was.

At first, I didn't think Katie had any interest in me. There was a misunderstanding when I ran into her at a supermarket near the hospital. She thought it was a bit strange that I didn't stop and chat. But it was just that, even in my thirties, I was still self-conscious about wearing glasses and embarrassed about how I looked after just getting out of bed.

Some time after that misunderstanding was sorted out, I asked her out for a bike ride and we hit it off. We started spending more time together.

Katie grew up in the Sutherland Shire in Sydney's south— her dad Michael was a GP and her mum Margaret had been a nurse—and she'd had a fascinating life that included travelling solo overseas. She was a keen reader, enjoyed bushwalking (like me) and theatre, played netball and other sports, and had a great group of friends. As I came to know her, I fell deeply in love very quickly.

Early in our relationship, we had a memorable trip to Nepal and India. After flying from Kathmandu to Lukla and beginning our walk to Everest Base Camp, we developed headaches. We took a diuretic drug called thiazide to help with symptoms of altitude sickness, and the next morning we each had another tablet.

As the morning went on, a guide we'd hired to carry a backpack was surprised by how vigorously Katie and I were charging up a steep climb. I eventually realised that instead of the morning dose of thiazide, I'd given us dexamethasone, a strong corticosteroid that treats bad cerebral oedema (swelling of the brain, which is one of the potentially fatal side effects of altitude sickness). It boosted our energy levels and sent us powering up that climb. For a doctor, it was a dumb mistake, but fortunately it didn't have serious consequences.

When we reached Everest Base Camp, following a path up through a series of valleys, it was spectacular. The magnificent mountains, the clear blue sky, the bracing air... everything was so stunningly beautiful.

India was such a vibrant, eye-catching and overpowering new experience, and having Katie share it with me—she'd been there twice before—made it the best holiday I'd ever had.

Back in Sydney, Katie and I, now committed to being together, were both super keen to have children. Having grown up with a community of relatives in Launceston, I'd long wanted a family of my own. I loved kids and could imagine how tremendous it would be taking them to the park, teaching them to swim and reading stories to them at night. We'd both reached a time in our lives—in our thirties—when we were ready.

As years go, 2004 was exceptional. Our first child, Emily, was born at RPA in March.

She was adorable. When we took her home, I couldn't believe how exciting it was—and how much fun—to have a child. Just caring for and playing with her—even getting up at night when she cried—felt like a special experience. And I was blown away by how fantastic Katie was as a mother.

I was 37—older than most first-time fathers—and it took time for me to get used to not being in control of my life, and to learn new skills. But I wanted to get everything right so that Emily could have the best possible life.

She was a good sleeper as soon as she was put down. We had a sporty pram—as well as what seemed like a truckload of items generously passed on by other parents—and soon got into the habit of taking Emily in it for walks. She was a delight as a baby, then just as much a delight as a toddler— joyous, outgoing and friendly.

Katie's mum and dad, who lived in Sydney, were besotted grandparents. My parents doted on Emily from Launceston, too.

When Katie returned to work three days a week as a locum pathologist at Prince of Wales Hospital in Randwick, her mum Margaret looked after Emily and they developed a strong bond. One of Emily's first phrases was a toddler's version of 'strawberry milkshake', which was her favourite order when Margaret took her to a Newtown cafe.

While I was undoubtedly spending too much time at work, it wasn't lost on me that Katie was supporting me by only working part-time when her pathology career was in its formative stages. Generously, she could see the value in what I was doing and encouraged me to take opportunities as they came up.

The same year Emily was born, the International Academy of Pathologists Congress was held in Brisbane. The organisers wanted a special focus on melanoma so I'd been asked to prepare a program for a day-long symposium. While it was a huge job to take on outside normal work hours— it also included guest-editing a special edition of the journal *Pathology* on melanocytic tumours—I was keen because of the value it would have for other pathologists. I invited experts whom I'd met around the world to speak at the course, including Marty Mihm and Alistair Cochran. It went really well, and these experts became friends. As my work as a diagnostician, researcher and presenter became better known, opportunities to collaborate on research and speak at international conferences exploded. It was in Brisbane that I met Professor Artur Zembowicz, who later asked me to be a guest faculty member at Harvard Medical School, talking about skin tumours at a course the following year.

That same year I was drawn into the history of melanoma treatment in Sydney after writing a paper that showed mitotic rate was a strong prognostic factor in the outcome for melanoma patients, second only to the thickness of the tumour. We decided it would be valuable to compare our findings with the data collected decades earlier by the late Vince McGovern, a pathologist at RPA, but there was a problem. Vince's findings were based on a score for what was called 'a high-powered field' (one field of a microscope under high power). Because every modern microscope had slightly different sized fields, our scores were based on the new standard of 'per millimetre square'. So, the only way we could compare the data was to find Vince's microscope and measure its high-powered field.

Fortunately, Helen Shaw, a veteran epidemiologist who had been hired way back in 1966 to collate the records of every melanoma patient since 1957, was still working at the Unit. Before computers, her job was a complicated exercise. Helen meticulously compiled a database on cards with holes punched in them. If she wanted to find all the patients with bad sun damage when they were diagnosed, she pushed a knitting needle through the cards to isolate those records. If she wanted patients with desmoplastic melanomas (a rare form of skin cancer), she pushed the needle through another hole.

It was basic but effective. When computers arrived, Helen managed the changeover and turned her work into an internationally recognised asset called the Melanoma Research Database. It generated insights that ultimately allowed improvements in defining the stages of melanoma: from Stage I for a thin, localised cancer to Stage IV for cancer that had metastasised around the body. It also allowed analysis of melanoma features that determined outcomes in patients, such as age, gender, site of occurrence, subtype and how patients had been treated.

While Helen seemed gruff when we first met, that was a misleading impression. She was a brilliant academic with a warm heart and a passion for melanoma research. She was sceptical that we'd find Vince's microscope, but she knew how to identify it if we did: it had a small plaque on one side that said it had been donated by a bowling club.

After asking everyone I could think of if they knew where the microscope might be, I learned that Vince had done some pathology work for a long-closed private laboratory after retiring from the Unit. With more calls, I tracked down the owner of the lab, which was based in a house at Dulwich Hill. 'Yeah, it's out there,' he said. 'Go and have a look.'

Arriving at an empty, run-down house, I was surprised to find two old microscopes still set up on a bench amid clouds of dust. One had a plaque on the side to say it had been donated by a bowling club. Bingo! Before I choked on the dust, I measured the high-powered field size and took a photo of the plaque to show Helen. Back at the Unit, we found that Vince's data validated our findings, and we published another paper on it.

Some people describe pathologists as medical detectives. Tracking down Vince's microscope was a different type of detective work.

———

As John Thompson and I collaborated on more research papers, he often came around to our house to help me with them on weekends. The number of papers I published jumped from eight in 2002 to fifteen in 2003, and then to thirty-three in 2004.

Another influential figure at this stage of my career was Professor Rick Kefford, a medical oncologist with a special interest in melanoma who had moved from RPA to Westmead Hospital. He suggested the Sydney Melanoma Unit aim for what was called a program grant—the highest tier of funding for important research—from the National Health and Medical Research Council, the Australian federal government body that funds medical research. While we had never had serious government funding before, our work was saving lives and, with more research, we believed we could save many more.

We formed a team to pitch for a grant under the aegis of the University of Sydney, with Rick as head. The other researchers—called 'chief investigators' in the application—were John Thompson (surgery), Peter Hersey (clinical immunology), Graham Mann (medical oncology/scientist) and me (pathologist). While including me was a risk, because I was easily the most inexperienced team member and each chief investigator would be scored as part of the application, the others thought I brought complementary skills and had a solid track record in research. Despite the workload, I was delighted to be involved.

We spent countless hours, often in our own time, writing up the proposal and practising interviews for our grant evaluation. Katie was very encouraging, taking on the extra load at home so I could refine our pitch.

If work was going well, so was life at home. Katie and I wanted to have kids who were close in age, so we were delighted when Matt was born, also at RPA, in November 2005.

He had a rough start, though, when he ended up in intensive care at Prince of Wales Hospital with a fever after just two weeks. After scans and a lumbar puncture, we were sick with worry when we learned he had meningo-encephalitis—a potentially life-threatening combination of meningitis and encephalitis. While Matt came through it, a paediatrician advised us that he could have permanent side effects, including hearing loss, which we wouldn't detect until he was two or three. Happily, that fear proved to be unfounded.

Matt and Emily, just nineteen months apart, loved each other's company. Katie had babysitting help from her mum when she went back to work part-time. We both had busy lives but we loved having kids, so it was a fulfilling time.

But we quickly realised our house in Newtown wasn't big

enough for a family of four. We had to move. Katie and I saw a house for sale in Petersham that we liked, so we made an offer and were accepted.

The next challenge was selling our existing house, hopefully quickly, so we weren't left with two mortgages. Katie stayed with her parents and the two babies while my dad and I fixed the Newtown place up ahead of an auction.

When we had open houses scheduled, Katie and the kids stayed at my parents' house in Tassie so we didn't have to keep making the place look perfect twice a week. Whenever the real estate agent told us we had a potential buyer visiting outside open-house hours, I would ride my bike home from work and make sure everything was as neat as possible. The day before the auction, we sold the house, so we managed to avoid becoming too financially stretched.

Matt was another very cute baby. Like his big sister, who he sweetly called 'Elly', he loved The Wiggles. When Katie took the two of them to see a show about ballerinas at the Sydney Opera House, Matt, who was just walking, made his way around other kids' backpacks, gently stroking The Wiggles' logo whenever he saw it. He loved to dress up as the Red Wiggle. It was a thrill for me as much as for Matt when he met Murray Cook, the original Red Wiggle, at a concert one day, with both of them wearing their matching red skivvies.

As Emily grew up, she loved dressing as a ballerina, dancing and putting on shows, much to everyone's delight. She tried to involve her little brother, who was just as chatty as her. Katie and I could hardly have been happier.

At least once a year, we'd go to Launceston to visit my parents, who were both retired. While Dad was in good health, Mum had had both hips replaced. With our growing brood, we spent lots of time with Katie's family as well, and they were very kind to us. On Sunday afternoons, her dad would bring around a tray of fruit and vegetables, which he'd bought at the markets. He'd come around as often as possible to spend time with the grandkids, putting Emily in the backpack and taking her for walks around the area to see birds and other inner west animal life.

Margaret, Katie's mum, also looked after the kids whenever we needed it. She loved them and it was clear they loved her back. We had regular get-togethers at Nicoll family houses—with Katie's sister Sally, her brother Charlie and his wife Sophie—and we would also go to restaurants together.

At work, we were delighted to find that all the effort on our pitch had paid off: we were awarded a five-year program grant worth $7.895 million from the National Health and Medical Research Council. It transformed our research. We employed two more people to continue building the Biospecimen Bank, and started the Australian Melanoma Genome Project, which used the Melanoma Research Database and the Biospecimen Bank to map the entire genome of 500 melanomas. It was a new scientific frontier for understanding and treating the disease, and it gave our work a new focus.

Shortly after we heard about the program grant, I had a message asking me to meet the dean of the University of Sydney's medical school, Professor Andrew Coats. I was deeply honoured when he invited me to be a clinical professor in the Faculty of Medicine and Health. It seemed crazy to everyone, including me, that I was a professor at 39, while Stan McCarthy—after his long and amazingly distinguished career—wasn't. So, with John Thompson's assistance, Stan was also made a professor. While as modest as ever, he was proud of the recognition and I was delighted for him.

In the next few years, there were giant leaps in melanoma work. In 2007, under the guidance of my friend and colleague Associate Professor Jon Stretch and businessman Reg Richardson, entrepreneur and philanthropist Greg Poche and his wife Kay Van Norton Poche donated a staggering $40 million to create a world-leading cancer facility for melanoma treatment, research and education. With their donation, the Sydney Melanoma Unit became Melanoma Institute Australia, a new name that gave the organisation a national profile, and more independence from both RPA and the University of Sydney.

At home, Emily and Matt got a gorgeous little sister. Two years after Matt, Lucy was born—also at RPA—in January 2008. It was the same day as my parents' 50th wedding anniversary and they'd come to Sydney to celebrate, so it was a busy—and exciting—time.

Lucy was a sweet and very loving baby who, before too long, proved to be a touch more adventurous than her older siblings when it came to swings and other playground equipment. Even before she could speak, she joined in all of Emily's and Matt's games and stories. They dressed her up and the three of them put on shows. The kids all shared a bedroom, with a toy room upstairs and another one downstairs. From the age of four, they all started piano lessons up the road.

It was intense with three young children and I continued to be in awe of Katie as a caring, fun and always upbeat mother. She was outstanding at teaching the kids to speak and read, and the right way to behave.

As happens for parents of young kids, we became friends with the parents of other young kids and our social lives soon revolved around children's parties and sport. I took them to swimming lessons, then swim squads at Leichhardt Park Aquatic Centre, and we became very familiar with inner-west parks.

When I had to head overseas for a conference, workshop or meeting, it was tough for Katie. If I had to miss dropping Emily at swim squad at 5.30 a.m., she had to load the three kids in the car, drop Emily off, collect her at 7 a.m., then, after getting them breakfast and ready for school, head to her three-day-a-week job as a pathologist at Liverpool Hospital in the south-western suburbs.

Life became progressively easier when our kids went, one by one, to a long day-care centre in Darlington. But if I was away, it still meant that Katie had to leave work early to pick them up by 6 p.m., which often meant going into the lab for an extra day to get through all her pathology work.

Around this time, I was offered an honorary role I couldn't refuse: lead pathologist for the Cancer Genome Atlas's melanoma project in the United States. It added to my workload in Sydney but was another internationally important role.

In 2010, the Institute moved into a new building called the Poche Centre, opposite the Mater Hospital in Wollstonecraft—the result of Greg and Kay Van Norton Poche's generous donation. There were four clinicians as founding members. John Thompson was executive director and Jon Stretch, a plastic surgeon who had been a friend since we'd socialised at the World Melanoma Congress in Venice, was deputy director. Rick Kefford, who'd become a good friend after we spent so much time and effort applying for our program grant, and I were the other two members.

But it wasn't long before another medical talent joined us at the Institute.

When she became part of our team, Georgina Long already had an impressive resume: after a PhD and post-doctoral fellowship in organic chemistry, she had studied medicine and qualified as a medical oncologist. She quickly made a mark with her passion, intelligence and commitment to getting the best results for patients, and her contributions to research.

Georgina and Rick started using the first effective drugs for what's called targeted therapy—attacking molecular targets on cancer cells. To study their effectiveness, Rick had earlier introduced an excellent program called Treat, Excise and Analyse for Melanoma (TEAM): a biopsy was taken, the patient was given the targeted therapy drugs, then there was a second biopsy to compare with the first. Georgina modernised the TEAM protocol.

Even though we understood a lot more about melanoma than we had even a few years earlier, Stage IV was still a terminal disease for the majority of patients. Once they were diagnosed, there was usually little an oncologist could do except advise them to get their affairs in order, enjoy what time they had left with their family and friends, then go into palliative care.

That was about to change.

When the world's first clinical trial of a targeted therapy drug called Dabrafenib commenced in 2009, Rick and Georgina saw astonishing responses from patients. I remember them coming into our multidisciplinary team meeting at the Poche Centre with huge smiles. After trialling treatments for advanced melanoma for decades without success, Dabrafenib, a so-called BRAF inhibitor, was being used to treat advanced melanoma patients who had a mutated version of a gene called BRAF V600—present in about 40 per cent of cases.

Rick said they had given Dabrafenib to patients who had come into the clinic in a wheelchair or who were confined to bed. Within days, some of them were getting back to work. 'It's ridiculous how quickly these drugs are having an effect,' he said.

It was astonishing news!

Dabrafenib was stopping tumour-cell proliferation caused by the mutated BRAF gene. When we examined specimens from patients who'd been treated with it, we saw that immune cells called lymphocytes had infiltrated these tumours. This drug was saving the lives of patients who seemed to be terminally ill.

What we had hoped—that advancing the science would transform the treatment of melanoma—was happening. After applying for a second program grant, with Professor Nick Hayward (genetics) joining as a sixth chief investigator, we received just over $12 million for five years starting in 2011.

Little did we know how much a new type of treatment called immunotherapy would revolutionise what we were doing.

Me and my older brother Mark mucking about together on the sun deck of our family home in Launceston when I was about four. Mark was a great older brother.

In November 1973, when I was six, I went on my first overnight bushwalk with a group of other kids and their dads, family friends of ours. This photo was taken at Hazards Beach, in Freycinet National Park, Tasmania. I'm the kid in the middle, wearing the blue t-shirt, and Mark is at the end on the right.

Every Christmas holidays my family would camp at the same site in Ulverstone, Tasmania. We all made friends with the neighbouring return campers, and we kids would roam the campsite with our mates.

Me and Mark in front of our family home in Launceston in August 1976. Mark is wearing the school footy team's colours and I'm in my beloved Hawthorn colours.

In December 1978, I travelled with my family to Johannesburg, in South Africa, only a few years after the Soweto riots. My parents took us to Soweto to understand what had happened. The kids there were incredibly friendly and joyful—and fascinated by my white-blond hair!

In November 1980, we celebrated Mark's sixteenth birthday. Mum had made one of her amazing pavlovas, which we had at every family celebration.

The first day at Riverside High School for me, entering Year 7, while Mark was about to start Year 9.

In 1982, I and my cousin (and close friend) Maree Pennington née Apted were appointed head prefects at Riverside High School.

I was always interested in sport and in May 1990, I was playing AFL for the 'Old Launcestonians' while I was a medical student doing a term at Launceston General Hospital.

In 1990, I graduated from medicine at the University of Tasmania. Nanna, Mum and Dad came to celebrate the event.

In 1991, after five cold November days hiking the Overland Track in the Cradle Mountain–Lake St Clair National Park, my friend Jon Morris, Dad and I reached Dove Lake at the northern end of the trail.

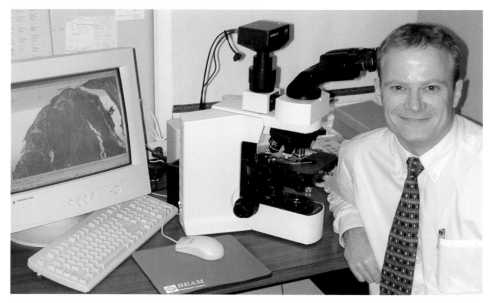

Technology has come a long way over the years I've been in pathology. In April 2002 I was using the first digital camera attached to a microscope at Royal Prince Alfred Hospital. The camera had been funded by the Melanoma Foundation.

Travelling with Katie in India, in December 2002. Seeing the Taj Mahal up close was an amazing experience. It was the best holiday I'd ever had.

Posing for a photo after I raced in the World Duathlon Championships in Adelaide in 2015. It was such a buzz having my family there cheering me on.

In Chicago in 2015, I had the fantastic privilege of representing Australia in the World Triathlon Championships Series, with my son Matt cheering from the sidelines.

In December 2017 the next generation of extended family gathered for a meal in Launceston. From left: Katie, Matt, Emily, Mark, Lucy, Dad, my sister-in-law Anna, Mum, my nephew Noah, me and my niece Maia.

In 2019, I introduced Emily and Matt to the Overland Track, and we are pictured here at the sign marking the end of our hike. We were fortunate to have very good weather for the whole trip.

In January 2020, we travelled around Europe, and here Matt, Lucy and Emily stand with me in front of the Colosseum in Rome.

In January 2021, Lucy and I did the Sydney Harbour Bridge Climb together and loved it.
(BRIDGECLIMB SYDNEY)

In 2021 I acted as a guide in triathlon qualifying events for my good friend and powerhouse athlete Trevor Murphy, who has a vision impairment.

In May 2023, Katie joined me in Poland and we enjoyed a stimulating hike with friends in the stunning Tatra Mountains . . . little did we anticipate the formidable new journey that stretched ahead of us.

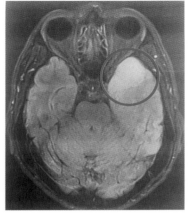

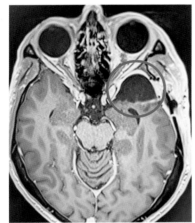

Top left: The day after our walk in Tatra Mountains, I lay in a Polish hospital after having my first seizure.

Top right: The Polish brain scan showed a mass in the 'left temporal lobe' (circled).

Left: On the brain scan taken almost a year later, after immunotherapy, anticancer vaccinations, surgery and radiotherapy, the dark area shows where the tumour had been.

Associate Professor Brindha Shivalingam has been a wonderful friend and is an incredible neurosurgeon, and she operated on me so skilfully twice in June 2023.

With my friends and colleagues outside the Poche Centre at Melanoma Institute Australia on 8 June 2023—the date I went public with my diagnosis. On the left are Matthew Browne (CEO) and Angela Hong (radiation oncologist), with Georgina Long (medical oncologist and co-medical director) and Jon Stretch (plastic surgeon and deputy medical director) on the right. (MELANOMA INSTITUTE AUSTRALIA)

In November 2023, the ABC filmed me with Katie, Matt, Emily and Lucy for an episode of *Australian Story*—another surreal experience along the way. Since being diagnosed, I've never been more aware of how much I love and appreciate my family. (AUSTRALIAN STORY/JACK FISHER)

From the beginning I have had regular immunotherapy treatments—including the triple agent immunotherapy I received in January 2024. Garry Maddox (co-writer of this book, triathlete and now friend) and Nurse Shanshan Zhang stand on either side of me.

I loved taking part in the Tour de Cure Signature Tour in March 2024, and I'm pictured here with my old friend Jim Finlay from Launceston and one of the amazing TDC Support Crew, Claire Robertson.
(CLAIRE ROBERTSON)

Back in February 2022, Katie and I went down to Government House Sydney, where I became an Officer of the Order of Australia (AO).

A little more than two years later, in June 2024, Georgina and I were humbled and thrilled to share the honour of being named the joint 2024 Australian of the Year by Prime Minister Anthony Albanese. (NATIONAL AUSTRALIA DAY COUNCIL)

In early June of 2024 Georgina and I were lucky enough to join an Australians of the Year 'Tour of Honour', which included a trip to the Yirrkala community in the Northern Territory. Front row from left: Georgina, Nova Peris (1997 Young Australian of the Year) and Yalmay Yunupingu (2024 Senior Australian of the Year); back row: Witiyana Marika (2024 NT Local Hero) and me.

A few weeks later, on a South Australian trip, Katie and I enjoyed a delicious lunch in the beautiful Barossa Valley.

In late June 2024 Katie and I attended the Amie St Clair Annual Ball in Wagga Wagga. Next to me is Sophie Nicoll (my sister-in-law, married to Katie's brother Charlie), and next to Katie is Josephine Reardon (Sophie's sister and a Wagga Wagga local).

On 20 May 2024, we marked, with dear friends and family, one year since my initial seizure in Poland that had led to the discovery of my glioblastoma. From left to right: Lucian Pearce, Charlie Nicoll, Nina O'Connor, John O'Connor, Sophie Nicoll, Sally Nicoll, Katie and me, Anthony Meaker, Michelle Meaker, Mark Scolyer and Anna Sublet.

7

A PENICILLIN MOMENT

After my brain cancer diagnosis, it became even more apparent that family—Katie, Emily, Matt and Lucy—was the most important thing in my life. I felt lucky that we were close, and that we'd had so many memorable times together.

When the kids were little, I loved taking them to playgrounds near our place. We would ride bikes, kick balls and fly kites. Other times, we would go for a swim at Leichhardt pool. At home, the kids would sometimes put on shows. We played Cluedo, Monopoly Empire, Ticket to Ride and other games, watched movies and sometimes went out for a hot chocolate. At night, Katie and I read them stories before bed.

When they were old enough, all three of them went to nearby Taverners Hill Infants School from kindergarten to Year 2, then headed to different primary schools in the area. They were active kids: Emily was a keen swimmer and took up ballet; Matt swam, played soccer and did kung fu; and Lucy also did ballet and played soccer.

Like many parents, we were happy they were growing up healthy. We hoped their education would give them opportunities to enjoy their lives, make the most of their talents and succeed at whatever they wanted to do. While their childhoods in the city were different to mine in Launceston, we took them to Tassie for at least two school holidays a year—to spend time with my parents and travel to some of the places I had loved growing up. Sometimes we camped; other times we stayed with relatives.

By 2012, life was busy with three kids under nine. I also had three strands to my work. How did we juggle everything?

It helped that I'd long been an early riser, typically not sleeping well and getting up at 4.30 a.m. I could be productive—getting cracking on work demands and research papers—while the household was quiet.

My main job by then was at the RPA Tissue Pathology lab, diagnosing difficult melanoma cases that had been sent to me from around the country and internationally, which I did on Mondays, Wednesdays and Thursdays from about 8 a.m. till 7 p.m. I carried out research at RPA and the University of Sydney on Tuesdays. I started Fridays by discussing the diagnosis and management of challenging cases at the multidisciplinary team meeting at the Institute's Poche Centre, across the Harbour Bridge, at 7 a.m. Then I'd go back to the RPA lab to work.

I tried to get home for dinner with the family every night, but I was often late, especially as my workload increased. Dinner and afterwards were good chances to chat to Katie and the kids. Then I'd crash early, heading to bed at 9.30 p.m., asleep by 10.30 p.m. When there was an urgent grant application that was due or a talk I had to give, I'd either stay back at work or stay up late, sometimes all night.

It was a lot to fit in, and my life would only get busier over the next decade.

I was passionate about my work, which put extra pressure on Katie, but she was always supportive. While I tried to pass on values to our kids that I believed were important, Katie, as well as taking on most of the household duties and having a pathology career, led the way in teaching them right from wrong, and the importance of being respectful, compassionate and polite. I'm very grateful for everything she did.

———

At the Institute, the focus was on reducing the rising death toll from melanoma and improving outcomes for patients. Clinical trials using Dabrafenib and other BRAF targeted therapies (later combined with what's called a MEK inhibitor, the next protein downstream in the MAP kinase intracellular signalling pathway) had continued showing exciting results for advanced stage melanoma patients whose tumour harboured a BRAF mutation. But many of those who responded had relapsed within a year.

Then came a landmark moment.

The first immunotherapy drugs were released and used in clinical trials. The early results were so stunning that it has been described as a 'penicillin moment' for melanoma treatment, with huge potential to treat many other cancers as well.

American immunologist James Allison and Japanese physician, scientist and immunologist Tasuku Honjo separately discovered techniques to treat cancer by what their Nobel Prize citation later called the 'inhibition of negative immune regulation'. In everyday terms, tumour cells put up barriers to stop the body's immune system attacking and destroying them. Allison and Honjo discovered ways to remove these barriers so the immune system could take over and kill the cancer cells.

A quick note on the science . . .

While standard cancer treatments had long included surgery, chemotherapy and radiotherapy, immunotherapy took a different approach. Allison and Honjo's discoveries led to companies developing drugs with such complicated names as Anti-CTLA-4 and Anti-PD-1—they have different proprietary names but I prefer to stick with the scientific terms—that turbocharged the immune system so it could destroy tumours.

It was far from the first time scientists had tried to harness the immune system to fight cancer. Peter Hersey, a veteran immunologist at the Institute, had been trying for decades. But the clinical trials of melanoma vaccines had never been as successful as everyone had hoped.

Immunotherapy quickly started working in the clinical trials that Rick ran at Westmead Hospital and Georgina ran at the Poche Centre. Initially, they tried Anti-CTLA-4 on patients with Stage IV melanoma who were near death. Nothing else had been successful, so it was a last roll of the dice.

While Anti-CTLA-4 took longer to work than BRAF inhibitors such as Dabrafenib, it had a dramatic impact—prolonging the life of some patients. Another immunotherapy drug that was developed later, called Anti-PD-1, had even more impressive results in clinical trials. It was more effective and patients had fewer problems with side effects than they had with Anti-CTLA-4.

That was an important development because, for all their brilliant effects, the toxicity of immunotherapy drugs could cause a wide variety of side effects, such as skin problems, flu-like symptoms, diarrhoea, coughs, breathing difficulties and neurological weakness or numbness. Other side effects, particularly inflammation of key organs, could be so serious that patients had to stop treatment.

After this initial success, the steps to be taken over the next decade included clinical trials that used these immunotherapy drugs on patients with earlier stage melanoma. Successive trials continued to produce positive results, initially *after* surgery (so-called adjuvant therapy) then *before*

surgery (neoadjuvant therapy). When I studied the pathological response in a tumour removed about six weeks after
neoadjuvant immunotherapy, I was blown away. For some
patients, the tumours disappeared and did not return within
two years. We had landed on a treatment that was changing
lives. I could see how much potential it had for patients with
other cancers.

As immunotherapy revolutionised melanoma treatment, there
were crucial questions to answer. How could side effects be
minimised? Why did some patients not respond to these new
drugs? How were these patients best treated? As oncologists
gradually became better at managing side effects, data showed
that immunotherapy was not as effective if was given after
certain drugs, including chemotherapy and steroids.

Still, the results backed predictions that these new drugs
could be as much of a medical breakthrough as penicillin.
Within a few years we had gone from virtually every patient
with advanced melanoma dying to some patients being
effectively cured. Astonishing! We were saving lives not just
in Australia but around the world.

Two other brilliant medical oncologists who had trained
with Rick joined the team, Associate Professor Matt
Carlino and Associate Professor Alex Menzies. Together
with Georgina, they ran more clinical trials that continued
to deliver amazing results. Then these drugs began helping
patients with certain types of breast, lung, head and neck,
bladder, bowel and stomach cancers as well.

It was always essential to get the diagnosis right, though. My own family experience showed that.

When I was eleven, a doctor told my dad he had a melanoma on his chest. It was cut out, along with a lot of tissue—5 centimetres of normal skin around the melanoma that went down as deep as the underlying pectoral muscle. Dad needed a skin graft from his leg to cover the hole. He was in pain from the graft for weeks and his chest always looked strange when we went to the beach.

Because his diagnosis meant I had a family history of melanoma, while I was a registrar at RPA I asked Launceston General Hospital to send me a copy of Dad's slides and pathology report. When I studied them, I could see he'd actually had a benign mole. The pathologist at the time had reported that, too, but not until the surgeon had already operated. It was shocking to realise that Dad went through the operation and all that pain unnecessarily.

When I told Dad on one of our family trips back to Launceston, he wasn't too distressed. He thought it was too long ago to get upset about. 'Oh well,' he said. 'These things happen.'

Happily, the standard of medical care has improved since the 1970s—and is much more uniform across the country now—but I still know of recent cases where misdiagnosis has meant patients have either died or had treatment they didn't need. It's why I've always worked hard to improve the accuracy of diagnosis and reporting of treatment-determining pathological features.

One thing I hadn't been working hard to improve was my health. I was in my early forties when I realised I needed to look after myself better. I was a bit overweight, my blood pressure was sometimes borderline high and, because there was cardiovascular disease on my dad's side of the family, I had to worry about my coronary arteries staying open so I could be around and healthy for my kids as they grew up.

With everything going on in my life, I hadn't been exercising. So I started jogging first thing in the morning. I couldn't believe how slow I was compared to when I was in my teens and twenties, but I stuck with it. It took me a long time to break 50 minutes for 10 kilometres. But I enjoyed gradually getting fitter and the way a session in the fresh air boosted my spirits.

Year by year, my workload seemed to be increasing. By 2013, I was being sent more than 2000 cases annually to review. While it didn't take long to diagnose a basal cell carcinoma and write a pathology report, it was a different matter for the complex cases I was reviewing after up to ten pathologists had been uncertain about the diagnosis. For each case, there was a pile of slides to study and report on, which took at least half an hour. They were extremely interesting cases, raised fascinating questions and were ideal subjects for research. But they were time consuming.

I saw this type of work as a public service more than a money-spinner, which was why private labs didn't do it. While I'd been offered multiples of my salary to join private labs, I preferred the public system. The cases were more interesting, I could do research and I wasn't working for a company that was trying to make money. I was able to make contributions like helping to refine sentinel node biopsies and excision margins around tumours, contributions that benefited melanoma patients. Later, I worked to learn more about the molecular genetic basis of melanoma so I could better predict outcomes for patients, discern why some patients responded better than others and improve treatments.

I kept working on research papers to push the under-standing of melanoma forward. I co-wrote 42 papers that were published in 2012 and another 46 papers in 2013—bringing the total to almost 300 papers in a decade. What tended to happen was that the more you published, the more people asked you to talk at conferences about what you'd learned, sought your opinion and invited you to take on influential roles.

In 2013, Professor Jeff Gershenwald, who was the chair of the Melanoma Expert Panel for the American Joint Committee on Cancer's manual *Cancer Staging Systems*, asked me to be vice chair. Jeff was a surgical oncologist from the M.D. Anderson Cancer Center in Houston, and I'd come to know him from discussions and spending time together at melanoma conferences and meetings around the world. The committee was revising the guidelines for staging cancers for the manual's eighth edition, due out in 2017, which would affect patients with all types of cancer around the world. In melanoma, they still went from Stage I for a thin, local-ised cancer to Stage IV for cancer that had spread around the body, but there needed to be new guidelines for grouping patients based on the latest research discoveries. The accuracy of cancer staging was critical in making sure patients received the right treatment.

It felt like a huge deal to be asked—I think I was the first pathologist and first non-American to be offered such a key role—but I wanted to talk over the positives and negatives with Katie and John Thompson. Being vice chair would add to my already busy workload. But Katie and John were both encouraging, so I accepted the offer and, working in different countries, we made major updates to the cancer staging guidelines.

The same year, I was appointed chair of the Melanoma Expert Panel for the International Collaboration on Cancer Reporting, which represented pathology organisations in the US, Canada, the UK and Australia. We published the first edition of *Invasive Melanoma Histopathology Reporting Guide*, which was used around the world, in late 2013. In Sydney, I delivered the Vincent McGovern Lecture at the Annual Scientific Meeting of the Australasian Division of the International Academy of Pathology, and was subsequently elected president.

Another international honour soon came my way. Having written with Stan and Kerry in 2004 a chapter in the book *WHO Classification of Skin Tumours*, published by the World Health Organization—which felt like a big deal because it was the international bible for skin cancer diagnosis—I was stunned to be asked almost a decade later to be one of the editors of the next edition. Wow! While it might not sound like a bestseller, it was a bible for the medical community around the world. I discussed it with Katie and we both recognised it would be time consuming, but it was a huge honour so I accepted. It was an important book that every pathologist around the world was going to use.

I was also busy travelling—delivering talks in Arizona (Dermpedia's Comprehensive Course on Soft Tissue Tumors), Scotland (Edinburgh Dermatopathology Tutorial), Hamburg (World Congress of Melanoma) and Brisbane (Global Advances and Controversies in Skin Cancer).

To minimise the time I was away, I flew in to each event as late as I could and left as early as possible. It was better for both me and my family if I was only gone for a short period. They had been generous, after all, in allowing me to take on these international roles and trips to share the findings we had been making in Sydney. To help me sleep, I would take sleeping tablets on flights and when I was overseas. I'm not sure how I was affected by jetlag, but I was used to operating without much sleep and always found it easy to get fired up for important talks and meetings.

Most of these trips were to Europe and the US but I occasionally went to China, South Africa and South America. If I went somewhere unusual, like Rio de Janeiro, the kids would be interested in hearing what it was like, though I'd sometimes only have been there for a day or two, with most of my time spent in a conference venue.

As the kids grew into teenagers, they competed in all sorts of sports, so there was a lot of ferrying them around before school and on the weekends. Emily played netball, ran, swam and raced triathlons; Matt played AFL, cricket and soccer, and ran and swam; and Lucy played netball, soccer and AFL, and ran, swam and rock-climbed. I took the kids to swim club at Leichhardt pool on Saturday mornings, and competed in races against them. It didn't take long for them to be way faster than me.

Being away on work trips made me appreciate the time I spent at home. I went for bike rides with the kids on weekends. I kicked the footy with Matt at the park and was sometimes boundary umpire when he played for Newtown Swans and Glebe/Newtown Bloodhounds.

I would drop Emily and Matt at a 5.30 a.m. swim squad at Leichhardt and I started running around the inner west's famous Bay Run instead of driving home to Petersham then back again in Sydney's ever-increasing traffic. After a while I saw a group running intervals around the 7-kilometre track and thought it looked like a good way to get fitter. I found out they were called Pulse Performance and were led by coach Dani Andres. I joined their sessions and became friends with a group of passionate runners, including Kieran White, Fraser Turvey, Anthony Meaker, Trevor Murphy and later Trevor Thomas. The kids also joined Dani's squad, and he sometimes took them on running camps during school holidays.

As my run times improved, I learned that some of the other runners were racing triathlons. 'Wow,' I thought, 'it'd be great to get back into them.' I signed up for some races in a sprint triathlon series at Kurnell. Katie and a good friend, Laura Jallier, came out to cheer. It was fun racing—getting a kick from swimming, riding and running on a beautiful course, pushing myself to see how well I could go, then the thrill of heading down the finishing chute.

Later I saw a photo that showed I was the only triathlete wearing a cossie instead of a wetsuit. While I'd just been interested in finishing a race up to that point, I'd always liked to improve at whatever I did so I decided to get a wetsuit and find a way to get faster on the bike. One problem, though: I was scared to ride on Sydney's busy roads.

The Institute's first melanoma pathology fellow, Ric Vilain, who also raced triathlons, came up with a solution. He told me about a smart indoor bike trainer called the Wahoo KICKR that simulated what it was like riding outdoors. 'Get one,' he said. I did—and it made all the difference to how strong I was on a triathlon bike leg. For a couple of years, it seemed like no one else had smart trainers, so Ric and I had an advantage at races. We set our sights on trying to qualify for the Australian age-group triathlon team for the 2015 world championships in Chicago.

Upsetting that plan was finding out I had a kidney stone on Christmas Day in 2014 while visiting my family in Tassie. Back in Sydney, I had to have an operation to remove it. While recovering, I decided to do a race in Canberra that was a qualifier for Chicago. I'd just have to go slowly and hope to pick up some points.

When I told Ric that hardly anybody had entered his age group, he jumped in his car, drove to Canberra and raced as well. Later, we were both named in the world champs team, which felt like an achievement. Like many sporty kids, I'd dreamed of representing Australia. It had taken a while, but it was finally happening. I ordered the Australian team shorts and polo shirt for the opening ceremony, and a green-and-gold race suit with 'Scolyer' on the front.

I took Matt, who was nine, along for the trip to Chicago, where I was competing in the 45 to 49 age group. We had so much fun. The city was full of triathletes from around the world who were buzzing about competing and seeing the sights between races.

I could not have been prouder representing Australia. With Triathlon Australia putting on a practice bike ride around Chicago and a team breakfast in a hotel, I met so many enthusiastic people with a love of the sport. It was a thrill marching with the Australian team in the parade of nations, then watching the opening ceremony in Grant Park next to Lake Michigan. The age-group races were the lead-in to the final event for the world's best professionals.

I raced three events: the aquathon (short swim, short run), the sprint triathlon (short swim, bike and run) the next day, and the standard triathlon (Olympic-distance swim, bike and run) two days after that. Having Matt along made the event even more special. The family of a teammate looked after him while I raced, and he stood beside the road loudly yelling encouragement and wanting a high five every time I went past.

After my races, Matt came along when I visited three leading American dermatopathologists I'd come to know well: Pedram Gerami in Chicago, the legendary Marty Mihm in Boston and Klaus Busam in New York. They were generous people who made Matt feel welcome when we went out for dinner. I didn't tell Katie at the time, but I nearly lost him at a train station in New York. After turning around to check the destination of a train that had just arrived unexpectedly, I turned back to the horror of seeing that Matt had stepped on and the doors had closed.

I just had time to mouth 'Get off at the next stop!' before the train pulled out. It was a long wait for the next one so I checked a map, ran out of the station and sprinted for what must have been 1.5 kilometres to the next station. I was so relieved to see Matt waiting for me on the platform. Phew! We hugged for at least three minutes, both of us with tears streaming down our faces. When we left the station, we held hands tightly.

A month later, I raced for Australia again at the duathlon world championships (run, bike, run), which were held in Adelaide, with ten friends from Pulse Performance. Katie, the kids and my parents came along to barrack. I was hooked. If representing the country in Chicago had been special, with Matt cheering, it was even better racing with friends and the whole family sharing the experience. Emily did a fun run and, impressively, she won it. She went on to race for the Australian triathlon team in 2023, and Matt joined her the next year.

Sport wasn't just about having fun, though. I was really proud of our kids when they joined a campaign to support Aboriginal footballer Adam Goodes, who had been booed by rival crowds so often that it probably drove him out of the game. Emily, Matt and Lucy took it on themselves to dress up in their Sydney Swans gear outside our house with a poster that said 'I Stand With Adam'.

It was always a joy when we could travel together. A favourite destination was the Gold Coast; the kids loved the theme parks—the dolphin show at Sea World, the rides at Dreamworld and the slides at Wet'n'Wild. We also holidayed in Noosa and went walking in the national park.

Katie and I liked long drives—they were good opportunities to talk—and the kids travelled well in the car. In 2014, we set off to drive all the way to Broken Hill, in the far west of New South Wales, and back. We didn't intend to camp on the way but had a two-person tent in our car just in case. When we made a late decision to stop one night near Coonabarabran, all five of us squeezed into the tiny tent. It was below zero degrees outside but we were jammed in so tightly that we felt warm. We played cards and games then, when it was time for bed, slept surprisingly well, head to tail. Everyone enjoyed the experience so much that we camped for a second night. Driving more than 2000 kilometres together turned out to be a memorable holiday.

For my 50th birthday, we went to the US west coast, hired a car and visited San Francisco, Yosemite National Park, Monterey, Los Angeles and Disneyland. Then, with our close friends Ann and Quinn Sloan and their kids Remy and Maddy, Katie and I took the kids skiing for the first time at Snowmass just outside Aspen. These driving holidays, spending so much time together on the road, brought us closer together.

———

At the Institute, there was always a lot happening. Having done excellent work with our first two program grants from the National Health and Medical Research Council, we pitched for a third, with Georgina as our seventh chief investigator. We were thrilled to receive $14.663 million for 2016–20, which would let us really build on the work that we'd been doing.

Then, in late 2016, it was the end of an era at the Institute—John Thompson retired as executive director. While he would still see patients and carry out research, John stepped back from running an organisation he had steered to become a world leader in melanoma diagnosis, treatment and research.

It never crossed my mind to apply for the job. For one thing, it would have been unusual to put a pathologist in charge of an organisation of surgical oncologists, medical oncologists and other clinicians. I was also content diagnosing difficult cases and conducting research. But then it was suggested that I share John's role with Georgina, whose excellent work treating patients and driving clinical trials had seen her become a professor of melanoma medical oncology and translational research. I thought there was a logic to us combining our skills—we both had backgrounds in science—and sharing the workload of running the Institute. It felt like an opportunity to make more of a difference for patients, and we both thought we could make it work.

I was anxious, though, about the impact it would have on my family. It would be a time-consuming job that would involve extra responsibilities. But Katie was very encouraging, so Georgina and I pitched our vision for the Institute to an interview panel of Australian and overseas experts. When I heard we'd got the job, my first thought was how much work it was going to be. My second was how exciting it would be to help shape the organisation.

Georgina and I officially started as co-medical directors on the first day of 2017, sharing offices at both the Poche Centre and the Charles Perkins Centre at the University of Sydney, where we have a research lab. We found that whenever there was an issue to resolve, we were able to have an open discussion about what was best. While we had different ideas at certain times—about research priorities or staffing issues, for example—we knew we were both working towards the same goals so we settled any sticking points quickly.

This new role compelled me to rethink my work life. That meant prioritising the extra demands on my time, becoming as efficient as possible, saying no to many additional invitations, giving up some personal time to take an increasing number of overseas trips and arrive home late for dinner more often. As a fellow doctor, Katie was proud of the success we were having at the Institute so, even if I worried about leaving her with more of the family workload, she was always encouraging.

At a strategy meeting not long after our appointment, we decided on a significant goal for the Institute: we would work towards reaching zero deaths from melanoma in Australia. While we weren't sure when it would be possible, we were on the way. With targeted therapies and immunotherapy, Australian deaths from melanoma had been declining after decades of steady increases. In 2013, more than 1600 Australians died from the disease. Three years later, it was down to around 1270. The five-year survival rate for patients with advanced melanoma had gone from 5 per cent to 55 per cent in a decade.

Did these added responsibilities, an expanding research program and the extra travel eventually take me away from my family too much? Years later, I think it did. Like most of my colleagues, I was acutely aware of the family times I'd missed. But I had a strong drive to do good for the community, and we were saving lives.

―――――――

Given how intense work had become, triathlons were a pressure release. I'd enjoyed competing for Australia so much that I did it again at the world championships on the Gold Coast in 2018. Katie and the kids came up to cheer for me that weekend. Then I competed again in Lausanne, Switzerland, with Georgina and fellow Institute pathologist

Dr Rob Rawson also racing, in 2019. It was always exciting representing Australia.

I often trained early in the morning before the household was up, which minimised the time it took away from family activities. It's true I have a competitive personality, but I also liked feeling fit and valued the friendships I made while training and racing.

Other than short trips for triathlons, our overseas family holidays were often pegged to wherever work took me. Katie and I, who had rarely travelled overseas as a couple since having kids, managed a holiday together when I spoke at a conference in Cologne in 2016. Along with Jane Dahlstrom, a friend since we had both been anatomical pathology trainees in Canberra, I was part of a bid to bring the International Academy of Pathology Congress to Sydney. We won the bid and, just as importantly, Katie and I had a great time away together.

As the visiting lecturer for South-East Asia with the Royal College of Pathologists of Australasia, I had a lecture tour in 2019 to Malaysia, Hong Kong and Singapore. The family met me in Singapore afterwards and we had a holiday at Club Med. I'd gone on a Club Med holiday to Noumea with my parents, Mark and the Frost family when I was thirteen, so I knew how good they were. In Singapore, we threw ourselves into all sorts of activities, including tennis, basketball, snorkelling, sailing, swimming and archery. We enjoyed it so much that we planned another trip to Club Med in Bali.

In 2019, the whole family went to the UK to spend Christmas with one of Katie's best friends, Jane Martin, and her husband Byron Byrne. We then flew to Rome, hired a car and had a spectacular time driving around. Instead of Coonabarabran and Broken Hill—as tremendous as they were—we travelled to the Amalfi Coast, Pompeii, Florence, Tuscany and Venice. Then we flew to Paris, where I was speaking at a conference. It was terrific learning about different cultures, sights and food with the kids. We all put on costumes to join in mock-medieval fighting with swords and shields in Rome. There can't be much better than seeing joy in your kids' faces, even if they're battling each other with ancient weapons. Then COVID hit.

That was a tough time for everyone pretty much everywhere. As healthcare professionals, Katie and I were able to keep working. But our research lab at the Charles Perkins Centre closed for an extended period in 2020, then again in 2021, with some of our research assistants redeployed to COVID testing sites for NSW Health.

The two COVID years were each different experiences for us as a family. In the first year, I would take the kids for a jog in the morning within the restricted zone allowed by the health authorities during lockdown, and we played games online with relatives in other states. Matt and I would kick the football and I'd go for bike rides with Lucy.

In the second year, we were in a rented house in Leichhardt, a short drive from our usual community in Petersham, while our home was being renovated. The kids did online learning together in the same room, then they often cooked dinner.

I was worried for Emily, who was studying for the Higher School Certificate, but she did well.

Once the country returned to a new post-COVID normality, Georgina and I renewed our lobbying for changes we felt were important to keep reducing melanoma deaths. Speaking at the National Press Club in Canberra in 2022, we called on sporting organisations to move games away from the middle of the day, change training times and provide portable shade structures.

It was disappointing for us that Australia had dropped the ball in preventing a skin cancer that was on track to kill 16,000 people, leave 350,000 living with a diagnosis of the disease and cost the nation $8.7 billion by 2030 unless action was taken quickly. Every level of sport, from grassroots to professional, needed to minimise the risk of sunburn by taking such measures as swapping caps for broad-brimmed hats, using long-sleeved UPF50+ playing kits and ensuring sunscreen was applied and reapplied.

We also called on social media organisations and influencers to stop normalising, glamorising and trivialising sunburn and tanning, noting that a TikTok stream on 'sunburn tan lines' had had more than 200 million views. Shortly afterwards, we had a win when TikTok in Australia announced it was banning videos that encouraged tanning and would add warnings about the risks of skin cancer.

––––––––

I felt proud whenever accolades came my way. But I always knew they reflected what the Institute had achieved, dating back to such pioneers as Gerry Milton, Vince McGovern, Bill McCarthy, Stan McCarthy, John Thompson, Jon Stretch, Helen Shaw, Peter Hersey, Rick Kefford and Graham Mann. Any success Georgina and I had—as we often said in speeches—was from standing on the shoulders of giants.

At the NSW Premier's Research Awards for outstanding cancer researchers, I won various honours, including the Professor Rob Sutherland Make a Difference Award for being 'the world's most highly cited melanoma pathologist' and leading groundbreaking work. The judges said my work had made a real difference to the management and survival of melanoma patients and the classification of skin cancers globally. It was an award I was particularly proud of, because it showed that what we did in Australia, and what I did, had an impact around the world.

I'd kept publishing papers with our incredible team of researchers and collaborators—73 in 2018, 56 in 2019, 78 in 2020—but more important than those numbers was their impact. Just as I was always learning from other papers, researchers around the world were drawing on our work and advancing everyone's knowledge of melanoma and other cancers. To get to zero deaths, we needed to keep making progress.

The Institute was continuing to do valuable work. The Melanoma Research Database had developed to include more than 60,000 records, and the Biospecimen Bank had tissue, bodily fluid and other samples from more than 10,000 patients. Both were resources that underpinned our research and were used in collaborative projects with colleagues around the world.

In 2021, I felt humbled to be appointed an Officer of the Order of Australia (AO) for distinguished service to medicine, particularly in melanoma and skin cancer, and to national and international professional organisations. There was another honour—completely unexpected—when the American Society of Dermatopathology announced that I'd won the Founders' Award; this was one of the few times it had been given to someone from outside North America in its four-decade history. It was to be presented at the society's annual dinner in Chicago in October 2023. I didn't know if my schedule would allow me to attend, but it was certainly appreciated.

Before that, though, there was a lot of work to do and a couple of other international trips. I was donning the Australian triathlon suit again to race in in Ibiza, Spain. Then I was going to Poland to speak at a conference and, with Katie, catch up with my dear friend Artur Zembowicz and his wife Margaret. I was looking forward to it.

8

THE RADICAL PLAN

As Katie and I flew into Sydney on 25 May 2023, after the shock of Poland, there was little doubt in my mind that I had a glioblastoma, the worst type of brain tumour. I knew it was incurable, and I was distraught and angry to be facing certain death.

The next seven weeks would be an intense round of medical appointments, consultations with specialists and family talks, with things shifting day by day. I cried a lot out of sadness, anxiety and fear—sometimes with Katie, sometimes by myself.

DAY 1

Georgina met us at Sydney airport and kindly drove us back to our home at Petersham. Katie and I were touched that our kids had made the effort to welcome us home with a delicious breakfast. Katie's sister Sally, who had been looking after them, was there as well. Expecting that time with my family would be measured in months from now on, I was struck anew by how wonderful they were. I loved them so much.

But even though I was finally home and surrounded by family, I felt tense. After breakfast with everyone and a quick shower and change, Katie and I headed to the Chris O'Brien Lifehouse, the cancer treatment and research hospital opposite RPA that was named after my surgeon friend who had died from glioblastoma in 2009. Georgina had arranged for me to be admitted under the care of Associate Professor Brindha Shivalingam, the head of neurosurgery at Lifehouse, to begin what was called the medical work-up—investigations to establish a definite diagnosis and develop a treatment plan.

The Lifehouse team re-ran the tests from Kraków: an MRI brain scan, a lumbar puncture and various blood tests. I had a long venous line (a flexible tube) connected to a vein in my arm so I could receive the antiviral agent acyclovir intravenously. Until I had a brain biopsy, the team could not discount the slim chance that I had herpes encephalitis.

But Brindha, a highly skilled and compassionate neurosurgeon, who I had worked with for many years at the Institute was 99 per cent sure I had a glioblastoma.

Then Georgina said something that gave me a spark of hope amid the despair: since we'd spoken when I was in Poland, she and the team at the Institute had been developing a plan for a radical treatment. It was something that had never been tried anywhere, something that would take what we had learned from immunotherapy in melanoma and apply it to my own cancer.

The plan was to try a combination of immunotherapy drugs to activate my body's immune system before an operation to 'debulk'—remove the bulk of—the tumour.

The standard treatment for a glioblastoma, which I was shocked to learn had not advanced since 2005, gave patients the chance to live as long as possible, with the best quality of life, before palliative care then death.

This type of brain cancer always came back, so the survival rate was zero. The median survival time was about twelve to fourteen months. The median time for the brain tumour returning after surgery—recurrence—was just six months.

Once it came back, the last few months of decline would be awful—I'd lose functions like speech and memory, experience massive side effects like nausea, vomiting and headaches, and possibly be confined to bed—so I wouldn't have much quality time left with my family.

While we'd been revolutionising outcomes for melanoma patients, glioblastoma treatment had lagged. It was incurable almost two decades ago, and it was still incurable.

My treatment would start with surgery to obtain brain tissue to confirm, on pathological analysis, that I had a glioblastoma, not herpes encephalitis, and define its subtype. Once confirmed, I would have surgery to remove as much of the tumour as possible without causing so much brain damage that I'd be left with a worse quality of life. Three to four weeks after the debulking operation, under what was called the Stupp protocol—named after Swiss-born medical oncologist Professor Roger Stupp—glioblastoma patients generally started six weeks of daily radiotherapy to the tumour bed, Monday to Friday, to delay the recurrence. They also had six months of chemotherapy with a drug called temozolomide as another step to slowing recurrence.

Having spent many hours researching glioblastoma and the potential use of immunotherapy since hearing what had happened to me in Poland, Georgina, who had pioneered the use of combination immunotherapy for melanoma patients with metastases to the brain, proposed that we try something very different.

I would have a combination of three immunotherapy drugs—Anti-PD-1, Anti-CTLA-4 and the newer Anti-LAG-3— and delay debulking surgery for as long as possible to give them the best chance of working. While a glioblastoma was a very different cancer, immunotherapy had helped Stage IV melanoma patients whose disease had metastasised to their brain. We also knew that immunotherapy before surgery for Stage III melanoma patients (when it has spread to lymph nodes near the primary tumour on the skin) was much more effective than after surgery.

As soon as I heard the idea, I was keen. It struck me— excuse the pun—as a no-brainer, based on what we'd learned in melanoma. Having helped develop a protocol to assess the pathological response to immunotherapy before surgery,

I'd seen the follow-up data on these melanoma patients. Knowing how well they had responded filled me with hope. I knew there were dangers, though. It might give me more time with my family. But it might also give me less.

There was a risk that the toxicity of three immunotherapy drugs together could result in side effects that would make my life miserable or even kill me much more rapidly than the estimated twelve to fourteen months if I took the standard treatment. And delaying debulking could allow the tumour to grow quickly and spread further in my brain, with disastrous consequences. But I knew it was the right thing to do. I wanted to push the boundaries, using science and our melanoma knowledge, and try something new.

Could it save my life? There might be a 5 per cent chance. It could be less than 1 per cent. I just hoped it was better than zero. Even though the chances were slim, immunotherapy appealed because I knew as a pathologist that glioblastomas sent out tentacles at their periphery that infiltrated the surrounding brain. That made it impossible to remove all the tumour cells with surgery or mop them up with radiotherapy or other treatments without causing major brain functional deficits. We needed a treatment that could hopefully teach my body's own immune cells to recognise and destroy the tumour cells while leaving my normal brain cells alone.

So it was a risk–benefit analysis. It was trying something rather than accepting the dismal outcome under the standard protocol. And the science we would generate could help future glioblastoma patients, too.

A big question was whether we could get a neuro-oncology team on board for such a radical plan. They would have had little experience administering immunotherapy and none in trying it before surgery on a glioblastoma patient. It was such a risky departure from the standard treatment that I knew it would be a challenge to get the right team working with us.

At Lifehouse, I was grateful to friends and colleagues who swung by my bedside over the next two days, including RPA social worker and family friend Nina O'Connor; a young surgeon who had been a fellow with us at the Institute, Dr David Coker; and the head of the Sydney Local Health District, Dr Teresa Anderson. It was good to see them. I was also visited by Dr Ann-Marie Crozier, who ran the Hospital in the Home service so I could continue the antiviral drugs for herpes encephalitis for as long as necessary.

Once Georgina came up with the plan to try immuno-therapy, she had discussed it with our brilliant colleagues at the Institute. She later said they had taken 'absolutely every bit of knowledge from melanoma' and thrown it at my tumour.

There wouldn't be anything done at Lifehouse over the weekend, so Katie and I went home on Friday night. She took leave from her job at Liverpool Hospital to help me through whatever lay ahead.

DAY 3

Trying to make the weekend as normal as possible for the kids, we went as a family to watch Lucy play netball. It must have been shocking for them to hear about my brain tumour, especially in such a clumsy way from the other side of the world. As Katie said, they would have been reassured to some extent that I was walking and talking, but they were obviously very upset.

We encouraged the kids to go ahead with any plans they had and to keep going to school. To be honest and open, we told them we were planning the potentially risky treatment of immunotherapy before surgery. I'm sure they were frightened but they trusted that we would make the right decisions.

As Katie and I started the long process of talking through the who, what and when of treatment, we were comforted by visits from Katie's brother Charlie and his wife Sophie, and Katie's sister Sally and her partner Lucian. Their familiar company was good for us. While we were happy to talk about what we were going through, I was reeling—by turns sad, scared, angry and tearful. I could eat but not with any enthusiasm.

I'd called Mum and Dad in Launceston, and my brother Mark in Melbourne, as soon as I could. They were understandably very upset. Nobody gave us the kind of encouragement that is often given to cancer patients, like 'You'll get through this.' Everyone knew the gravity of what I was facing. No one we told about the treatment said, 'Don't do it.'

There were the first of many discussions with doctors both in Australia and overseas, and a nurse visited at home to give me the first daily intravenous infusion of antiviral drugs.

An incredible group of friends rallied around us, creating a roster to provide evening meals every day and helping take the kids to their activities. It would take a community to get us through those tough early weeks.

DAY 5

On Monday morning, we went back to the outpatients clinic at Lifehouse for the first of our meetings with specialists in neuro-oncology, radiation oncology and neurosurgery to seek their advice about the radical plan. Then we began visiting other hospitals to talk to more specialists.

Georgina had been busy organising calls and Zoom meetings with brain-tumour experts around Australia, Europe and the US to hear their opinions and ask questions. While we wanted our decisions to be driven by data, research on immunotherapy before surgery for brain tumours was almost non-existent.

Immunotherapy had been given to small groups of patients with recurrent brain tumours—ones that had come back *after* surgery—following radiotherapy, chemotherapy and often high-dose steroids, rather than *before* surgery as she planned. We knew from our work in melanoma that, after chemotherapy and steroids, immunotherapy was much less likely to be effective, so the lack of success in brain cancers that had recurred after surgery and other treatments was not surprising. As far as we knew, combination immunotherapy had never been tried before surgery on a patient with my type of brain cancer.

Some medical oncologists who Georgina, Katie and I had spoken to were reluctant to abandon the standard treatment for an experiment. My view was that even if it didn't help me it would likely lead to science that could help improve outcomes for future brain cancer patients.

Georgina called a meeting of the translational research team at the Charles Perkins Centre, which we co-led, to discuss how laboratory research could be performed on my tumour. Giving their insights at this meeting and subsequently were cancer-cell biologist Professor Helen Rizos, Biospecimen Bank head Nicole Caixeiro, medical oncologist Associate Professor Inês Pires da Silva, researchers Associate Professor James Wilmott, Dr Ismael Vergara and Associate Professor Mainthan Palendira, and many other talented and dedicated scientists and doctors.

While Georgina knew it would be tough for her to push for a non-standard treatment for a close friend, she said Helen gave her confidence when she immediately gave her opinion, as a scientist, that it was a compelling idea—that it wasn't just an opportunity, it was an *obligation* for us to try something groundbreaking.

Everyone recognised that this treatment was only possible for me because of a unique combination of factors: I was a scientist who knew the risks and was willing to try something that might kill me much earlier than the standard protocol; I hadn't quickly had debulking surgery when I'd been diagnosed; I was willing to delay this operation at further risk; I hadn't had steroids or chemotherapy; and

I had extensive knowledge of immunotherapy, including its potential benefits and risks.

The team at the Institute started the long process of fleshing out the positives, negatives and practicalities of my treatment, and working out how they could perform the kind of high-quality research that might change brain cancer treatment.

One key issue to resolve was how to get hold of the immunotherapy drugs Georgina proposed to use, given they were not approved for treating brain cancer in Australia. Georgina applied to the Therapeutic Goods Administration, the federal government agency responsible for approving medicines, to use the drugs because of my terminal condition.

She also approached an American pharmaceutical company with another innovative proposal: could they make me a personalised cancer vaccine, based on analysis of my tumour? If so, we reasoned, this could be another way to mobilise my immune system to attack the cancer cells.

As desperately as I wanted immunotherapy to work, I could see, as a clinician and scientist, that there was a very high chance that it would not. Compared to melanoma, glioblastoma has a low tumour mutation burden (the number of gene mutations in cancer cells), which usually means there are fewer neo-antigens (proteins derived from the cancer on the surface of tumour cells) that the immune system might be able to recognise and attack. There were also few, if any, tumour-infiltrating lymphocytes within it (known as TILs, these are immune cells within the tumour that are likely recognising the cancer cells and trying to mount an immune response against them).

I was scared, anxious and fearful that the glioblastoma would give me a horrific last few months, and leave Katie without a husband and our kids without a father.

But I didn't want to die. I loved my life. It felt right to have a crack and see if we could change the thinking about brain cancer.

I wanted Katie and me to drive all the decisions about my treatment. That meant asking lots of questions during our consultations with medical experts—many of them friends—both in Australia and overseas. If they themselves had a brain tumour, I wanted to know, who did they trust? How much of the tumour would they recommend removing? What brain structures should we keep in place? What were the chances of residual tumour being mopped up by radio-therapy? How much radiotherapy did they recommend? What damage could radiotherapy cause? How beneficial was chemotherapy? How might so-called novel treatments like immunotherapy and a cancer vaccine fit in?

Katie was a rock, taking notes during meetings to keep track of the advice we were getting. Despite the severe stress we were under, she was remarkably calm. As a doctor with neuropathology and clinical experience, her insightful questions made me especially grateful she was by my side.

I knew, as a pathologist, that a core biopsy (extracting a core of tissue) would not provide enough tissue for the intensive research we wanted to do. Discussing options with

Brindha, I was adamant I wanted a craniotomy for an open biopsy, where a section of skull bone is removed to take out some tumour tissue, then replaced. While this type of biopsy carries a marginally higher risk of an infection, Brindha did not need convincing. She was used to open biopsies and, knowing glioblastoma was incurable, she recognised the value of research that might give future patients a chance.

Every day I had up to four medical appointments, as well as discussions in person, on the phone or online about treatment. I was still struggling with the emotions around my diagnosis—scared and teary at home—but I did my best to focus on getting the most from these meetings.

Georgina had been planning to attend the American Society of Clinical Oncology's annual conference in Chicago to deliver two melanoma talks. She decided to make it a shorter trip that, as well as delivering her talks, would allow her to go to other sessions to learn about brain cancer and talk to glioblastoma experts. She came back saying that many of the medical oncologists she met sounded very positive about the approach we were planning to try.

But there were so many unknowns.

While there was no published data at this stage on whether it was better to give three immunotherapy drugs together to treat any cancer, it made sense that if you had a tumour that was unlikely to respond to immunotherapy, you would hit it with the big guns as hard as you could.

Data indicated, though, that there was a more than 60 per cent chance of what are called major adverse events—serious side effects from treatment—with Anti-PD-1 and Anti-CTLA-4. I would likely be at an even higher risk given I would be getting Anti-LAG-3 as well. And an even higher risk than that because we were dealing with brain cancer. If immunotherapy caused major swelling in my brain, it could kill me within days. Many neurologists were very concerned about this risk.

I knew as a pathologist that glioblastomas always came back because they sent off tentacles from their periphery into other parts of the brain—and these tentacles were too hard to detect, either by scans or by a surgeon during an operation, so the tumour could never be fully removed.

When one American surgeon told us he was confident of removing 98 per cent of the tumour, I was wary. The more tumour that was removed, the higher the risk that I would be left with reduced mental functions. My tumour was in the left temporal lobe, extending into the amygdala, which controls personality and emotions, and was also in the hippocampus, which affects memory.

Brindha was clear that preserving my mental functions would give me the best quality of life after the operation. If she tried to remove everything she could see on the scan, I might be so mentally deficient that I would not enjoy what time I had left, and might not be able to make decisions about my treatment.

Whenever there was resistance to our plan from doctors and I found myself getting angry, Katie was a voice of reason. They were being understandably cautious about a never-been-tried treatment that could kill a patient more quickly than the standard Stupp protocol. But I thought that if they knew as much about immunotherapy as we did, they might see what it could offer. Despite the risks, it gave me a slim chance—probably a very slim chance—of surviving.

Katie and I also had practical issues to deal with. We talked to our lawyer and to our banks, life insurance, medical insurance and financial advisors to make sure my affairs were in order and my will was up to date. Any major operation, particularly in the brain, was a risk. If I wasn't around, I needed to make sure Katie and the kids were looked after as well as possible. Down the track, I'd be offered cancer psychologists to help me deal with the emotions I was going through. For the moment, I was doing my best.

I zeroed in on what I needed to know. Katie said she'd never seen me more driven, firing on all cylinders. I had to be the person who made the decisions, who convinced the medical community that this was what I wanted and that I understood the risks.

DAY 12

On the morning of my biopsy at Lifehouse, I hugged the kids. They wished me luck and said they loved me before Katie and I left. She drove us to Camperdown and parked underneath the building. We both knew things could go wrong in a brain operation so, before we got out of the car, we hugged and said how much we loved each other. On the way to admissions, I ran into a doctor colleague from RPA who was being treated for prostate cancer. He hadn't known about my diagnosis—nor I his—so we exchanged warm wishes.

While I was anxious about the small chance of brain damage, there was no other option in my mind. If we were going for immunotherapy before debulking, and if we wanted data so that research could advance brain cancer treatment, it had to be an open craniotomy.

Over two hours, Brindha cut out about a fifth of the tumour, including some high-grade cancer that looked worse than other parts on the scans. It went smoothly. Brindha later admitted she was nervous operating on a friend and colleague, but she didn't give even the slightest hint of that to me at the time.

When I woke drowsily in the post-op recovery room, with a dressing covering a 15-centimetre incision on my left temple, I realised—from knowing where I was and how I was thinking—that I was still my usual self mentally. I had a pleasant conversation with a nurse who was looking after me. I was thrilled to see Katie when I came out. She was delighted that I'd come through the operation okay. I rang the kids, who were also happy, and they came in to see me later.

I stayed in the intensive care unit overnight. Even though I was on sick leave, I felt well enough later to check my emails, and I sent a complimentary message about the nurse to her boss.

The worst part of my recovery was the intense stinging from a urinary catheter that went into my bladder through my penis. When Brindha came round later that day, I was relieved that she said it could be taken out.

While physically recovering from the biopsy was one thing, dealing with the emotions of a terminal diagnosis was proving to be another. I was finding it overwhelming at times that I might have only months to live. That my kids would grow up without me. That the rich life I'd had before I left for Poland had been ripped away. I was fearful about what the future held and when down the track the cancer would come back.

I cried. I got angry. I felt sad. I cried again.

In time, I came to understand how difficult that period was for Katie and the kids as well. Their lives had been overturned, too. They hoped I would survive, but we all realised it was more likely the tumour or the side effects of my treatment would kill me. Fourteen months—the outer limit of median survival of twelve to fourteen months—would be July 2024. That wasn't very far away.

I really appreciated the support from everywhere that I was getting. Friends and colleagues from Sydney and around the world, including the MD Anderson Cancer Center in Houston, generously bought me a large-screen TV as a distraction during treatment. When I came home from Lifehouse, I watched some comedies on it with the kids.

I had been open and honest—that phrase again—with them since we arrived home from Poland, explaining about my brain tumour and the treatment. I answered any questions they had, like how long I was going to live, how much pain I would have and what we could do together. But after the operation, we were able to play some games and chat about our favourite holidays, which helped. I wanted to enjoy their company while I could.

DAY 14

The pathology confirmed I had a brain tumour but the result was even grimmer than expected. I had an aggressive Grade 4 IDH-wildtype glioblastoma. And every molecular feature of my tumour was bad—in medical terms, it was unmethylated with pTERT mutation, EGFR amplification and PTEN deletion, and expressed p53—which made it even more aggressive. In everyday terms, I had the worst type of glioblastoma.

It was sausage-shaped, about the size of a squeezed golf ball, and lethal.

As shocking as the diagnosis was, Katie reminded me there was a lot that was lucky about my situation. I was fortunate that I hadn't needed brain surgery while I was overseas. That I hadn't had to take steroids, which would have reduced the effectiveness of the immunotherapy drugs we planned to use in my treatment. That the tumour hadn't reached parts of my brain that could have left me mentally or physically incapacitated.

I was lucky that, as scientist, pathologist, clinician and co-medical director of the Institute, I understood immunotherapy, including how it worked on patients with metastases to their brain, the extent of side effects and its greater effectiveness when given before surgery to remove a tumour.

I was also lucky that, despite the distress, I was thinking clearly enough to make informed decisions about my treatment, with the advice and backing of a brilliant medical and scientific team around me. And that I had supportive family and friends.

Not least, I was lucky to have the support of Georgina as my medical oncologist when it came to resolving such issues as the medical hurdles to sourcing and administering combination immunotherapy and managing potentially disastrous side effects. Every one of these advantages made it possible for me to be the first patient to try something that would hopefully revolutionise brain cancer treatment.

All true. But I was still desperately sad that I had a brain tumour that would almost certainly kill me.

My treating team wanted to make absolutely sure I was aware of all the dangers ahead. I was asked how I felt about the risk—as low as it was—of dying in three months. That was okay, I said—I'm going to die anyway! I hoped it wouldn't happen but I was realistic enough to know it probably would.

Having talked through all the potential risks and benefits of the proposed treatment, Katie backed my decision to go ahead. While she'd had to comfort me a lot, she was facing a crisis, too—the loss of her life partner, the father of her children. The kids also recognised that, for all the risks, the radical treatment was the right option. They knew how successful immunotherapy had been for melanoma; maybe this was the moment to discover it would be effective for glioblastoma as well.

Ultimately, it would take courage for all of us to go down such an experimental path.

When Katie and I visited Brindha in her rooms, we discussed the timing and extent of the debulking operation. In melanoma, there is a six-week gap between neoadjuvant immunotherapy and surgery but Brindha felt this was too long given how highly aggressive my tumour was. She thought it could double or even triple in size in that time, which could result in seizures, memory problems and emotional and personality issues. The tumour could even spread so far that it would become inoperable and kill me within weeks.

We compromised on twelve days between immunotherapy and operation.

Brindha and I agreed that she would be conservative in how much of the tumour she'd remove. She would perform what she called a safe maximal resection, which would leave parts of the tumour behind to preserve as much as possible such important functions as memory and emotional control.

DAY 15

After telling medical colleagues about my diagnosis, I had been swamped by hundreds of texts, emails and messages that expressed concern, love and kindness. There were so many that a few days earlier I had decided to go public with my diagnosis on social media as a way of keeping everyone informed about what was happening while I focused on strategic decisions about my treatment. I'd had a Twitter account since I started as co-medical director of the Institute, sharing information about our work, and an Instagram account that I used to follow triathletes.

One of my colleagues thought that revealing my diagnosis publicly wasn't wise, and that it could affect my future job prospects. But I was more distressed about staying alive than risking a future job. I also felt my experience and skills meant that, if I somehow came through this, I wouldn't have trouble finding work. Katie and the kids were supportive, so I went ahead.

There was another reason I thought social media was a good idea. Most likely I was going to die before too long, so I wanted a way for my kids to remember me—watching the videos in the future—and hopefully be proud of what I was doing. It would be like keeping a diary for them.

I posted a tweet, addressed to friends and colleagues, with a photo outside the orange-brick entrance to the Institute. It said that I had been lecturing in Poland for Dr Artur Zembowicz two weeks before, with Katie, when I had had a seizure. My MRI scans had shown a temporal lobe mass and I was having a biopsy for what appeared to a glioblastoma grade 4. I ended with: 'Thx 4 kind wishes/support!'

It had 93,000 views and triggered media interest in what I was going through. The Institute set up a Facebook page called 'My Uncertain Path' and an Instagram account so that my posts could be shared on these platforms.

Georgina followed up with a tweet of her own: 'I will be there every step of this journey with all the life force I can bring, along with friends, family, colleagues and @MelanomaAus. Thanks to our national and international colleagues bringing their best ideas to this #glioma problem.'

I wanted to use these social media channels to document my cancer journey and draw attention to both melanoma and brain cancer.

We still faced the challenge of finding a neuro-oncology team, including a neuromedical oncologist and a radiation oncologist, who would manage my treatment. The difficulty getting them on board was that they didn't have much experience with immunotherapy drugs and would also be concerned about the potential life-threatening risks.

With Katie's help, I wrote a 'To Whom It May Concern' letter, signed by the two of us and a justice of the peace, confirming that I'd been actively involved in discussions about treatment options. It was a practical step that detailed our attitudes to Georgina's plan.

'As co-medical director of Melanoma Institute Australia and as co-author of many of the seminal papers on the use of immunotherapy treatment for melanoma, I am well informed on the mode of action, efficacy and toxicity of immunotherapy for melanoma,' I wrote. 'Given the dismal prognosis for the type of glioblastoma I have, and given the lack of treatment options which would have any significant impact on increasing survival and prognosis, I have actively pursued the opportunity to try immunotherapy for my disease.'

The letter said I had consulted with experts around the world, accessed the latest research and was aware there was a significant likelihood of toxicity from immunotherapy that might affect both my treatment and my overall long-term health.

'I'm aware that there is a chance I may die earlier after having had the immunotherapy than I might have if I followed conventional treatment pathways for glioblastomas,' I continued. 'My opinion is that it is worth taking the chance given the dismal prognosis ... and the chance I could die or be significantly incapacitated by the tumour in a short period of time anyway.'

I finished the letter by thanking the team of specialists who were giving me the chance to have immunotherapy, and expressing 'my hope beyond hope' that it might improve what short life I had left and help find pathways for future patients with aggressive glioblastomas.

A week later, amid discussions with neuro-oncology teams from Lifehouse and Royal North Shore Hospital in St Leonards, Katie and I wrote a second letter. This was more emphatic, and covered the course I wanted to be followed if surgery and my other treatments left me unable to consent at the time.

'I acknowledge that there may be times post-operatively when, due to some cerebral swelling or other impact, I may not be able to form the words or that I may not be of sufficient mental capacity to convince others that I am capable of giving consent, which is why I am writing this letter now,' I wrote.

I set out what I would like to have administered at appropriate times during my treatment, including additional doses of immunotherapy, vaccines, TILs therapy, modified TILs, CAR T-cell therapy, molecularly targeted therapy, checkpoint inhibitors and other immunotherapies.

'In the coming weeks I am also open to any new or novel treatments for glioblastoma which the medical and scientific team at [the Institute] and elsewhere may have come across through their scientific analysis of my tumour,' I wrote.

Katie signed the letters as reassurance that she was backing my wishes about this proposal if things went badly.

The team was finalised: I went with the neuro-oncology duo from Royal North Shore Hospital—medical oncologist Dr Helen Wheeler and radiation oncologist Associate Professor Michael Back. They were supportive of me receiving immunotherapy and had vast experience treating brain cancers. They also had collegial personalities and a strong team around them, particularly nurse practitioner Marina Kastelan. I was pleased that we'd solved another problem on the way to starting treatment.

DAY 16

I wanted to thank my colleagues at the Institute for what they were doing for me, so I went to the multidisciplinary team meeting at 7 a.m. and spoke to them. I'd delivered thousands of speeches over the years but, with all the emotion of my diagnosis and treatment, I was nervous.

Speaking from the heart, and close to tears, I told them that I was proud of what we'd achieved as a group. While some people had been concerned when Georgina and I became co-medical directors—because we weren't surgeons like past leaders, and we were sharing the role—the Institute had gone on to have a huge impact in Australia and around the world.

Everyone had got behind us and we had revolutionised treatment, research, knowledge of melanoma and outcomes for patients. I was optimistic that I'd still be working with them during my treatment. The speech got a warm reception from colleagues I considered friends. When there was a chance, I also wanted to thank the nurses at the Institute who were caring for me, including clinical nurse consultant Kate Willis from Georgina's team.

Shortly after the meeting, Katie and I crossed the road to the Mater Hospital, where I was admitted for the day under Alex Menzies, a medical oncologist colleague from the Institute. I had been co-supervisor for his PhD.

While excited to be getting my first dose of combination immunotherapy, I was also nervous about going into uncharted territory: how quickly would I have complications, I wondered, and how would I handle them? I felt better after Alex explained what the side effects often were, what to look for and what I should do if I developed any symptoms.

I was connected to an IV drip and the infusion began. While it felt a little cold at first, it was a smooth process that took four hours. I spent much of the time talking to visitors, including Georgina and the nursing staff who ran the clinical trials across the road. They swung by to monitor me and chat about what I was going through.

The first night at home I was fine. The second night I started having side effects: high temperatures—over 40 degrees—and vomiting in the middle of the night. The symptoms came and went suddenly.

I also developed a rash around my body, which I scratched, tearing some skin on my lower legs. I used creams to clear up the rash and realised I had to be more careful about not scratching. My hair and skin and the fluids on my eyes became dry, and I developed a runny nose.

When I had blood tests, my liver-function results showed that some of the enzymes were high. Hepatitis was a common side effect of immunotherapy and could lead to liver failure if it was not monitored carefully. The next dose of immuno-therapy was held back until my liver-function tests returned to close to normal.

DAY 18

In the late morning, I eased back into exercising with a walk and light jog of half a kilometre, which took just over seven minutes. I proudly posted it on the social media fitness app Strava as '1st walk since brain cancer surgery!'

Medical and triathlon friends posted messages of encour-agement. 'Go Dad!' Matt wrote.

I was feeling good so I walked/jogged another 2 kilometres at 5 p.m. That took me more than twenty minutes.

I wanted to get back into running. I felt like my life had been stolen from me and I was keen to reclaim some of it. It was good for my spirits as the endorphins kicked in.

DAY 24

The Institute hosted a party at our house for family, friends and colleagues before the debulking operation the following week. The guests included my brother Mark and his partner Anna, who had come from Melbourne; Brindha; Institute chief executive Matthew Browne and other members of the team; my long-time friend and research mentor John Thompson; my old friend Jim Finlay, who had travelled from Launceston; and some of my cycling and running buddies.

On that chilly night, I made a speech with my arm around Katie to thank everyone for coming, and saying what a tough few weeks it had been for us since the seizure in Poland.

'I'm not ready to die yet,' I said, my voice cracking with emotion. 'I'm keen to try and forge a new path, just like what we have done in melanoma over the 25 years that I've been working in the field.'

I struggled to hold it together as I spoke about the treatment. 'It's a long shot but from my perspective it's a shot I want to take,' I said. 'A miracle might happen for me and, if it does, it will then flow on for many other patients. I haven't had a good chat to Brindha yet about what I'm going to be like after surgery on Wednesday but I guess there's a chance that I'll lose my faculties from having a big chunk of my brain chopped out. So it felt like a good opportunity to have a get-together tonight.'

When I lost my train of thought, I joked that 'I've got a brain tumour; I'm allowed to forget things every now and again.' Everyone laughed.

I thanked Katie for her dedication and kindness in helping me to navigate a difficult journey.

'I'm not the easiest person to live with at times,' I said. 'I'm very driven. I can't help myself. I've got to push myself with exercise and our research and all the rest of it.

'Katie is the kindest person I've ever met in my life. She sacrifices so much to support me and she's there as a confidant. When dramas happen in my life and I need someone to talk to, no matter what, Katie is always there and I can never thank her enough for what she's done.'

I also thanked Georgina for her leadership and friendship. In a speech of her own, she was kind enough to say what a special person I was and how amazing my family was.

'How wonderful it is to be able to celebrate tonight and recognise all the contributions you've made to melanoma but, even more importantly, your leadership and your mind and how you've encouraged all of us,' she said. 'It's a difficult thing to deviate from what the medical community would think is standard, even though we know the standard treatment for your glioma is extremely poor with not a great prognosis.

'So you are brave, you're courageous, you're an example to us all. I want to say how honoured I am to walk by your side, and that of Katie and the family, to help you with this journey, and how grateful, so grateful, we are to have the colleagues we have.'

Georgina finished by saying how much we'd learned about glioma in the last three weeks: 'It's crammed all of our melanoma knowledge into three weeks on glioma. Our international colleagues have been wonderful, have given us their time, have met with us in these three weeks to educate us about glioma.

'This is the right place to do this. We were just saying the plan we've put together with our colleagues is the right plan. It's spot-on. It's a real hope. The odds are against us but it's a real hope. And that can only be because of the wonderful people we work with.'

I was grateful for a beautiful night.

It was special that the kids were there to get a sense of the treatment we were going for and the brilliant medical community that was galvanising around us. We had tried to have as much normality at home as possible, with Matt and Lucy going to school and taking part in their usual sport and leisure pursuits. Emily, who had taken some time off from studying in Canberra to stay in Sydney, had been generous to the whole family. She had been driving Lucy to school and other activities, shopping, tidying up and organising meals and study schedules.

When we spoke to Matt and Lucy's schools about what the family was going through, they were exceptionally support-ive. Matt was coming up to the Higher School Certificate, with important assessment exams in the coming weeks. The school said that if he could sit these tests, he would get his HSC even if things went badly for me medically and he couldn't do the final exams.

It wasn't easy for Matt but, to his credit, he did really well. All three kids were amazing during a difficult time.

DAY 27

I posted my first video on X, with Katie at our home, to update people that I felt good after my neoadjuvant immunotherapy treatment and that Brindha would operate to debulk the tumour the next day.

'I'm scared for what the future holds for me,' I said. 'But I'm thrilled about the support that I've had from my colleagues and indeed people around the world as I embark on my cancer journey. And, I guess, in truth what I'm partly excited about is hoping above all hope that maybe the incredible discoveries that we've made in melanoma can be utilised to improve brain cancer.'

DAY 28

On a cool morning—I needed a Huskisson triathlon hoodie and a coat to keep warm—Katie and I drove to RPA and walked into the hospital holding hands.

We headed downstairs to admissions, joined the line and signed the paperwork for me to be admitted. After a while I was called out, kissed Katie goodbye and went through to change into theatre undies, a white gown, stockings for my feet and a blue surgical cap. I had worked at the hospital for 25 years but this was a new experience.

While I was in the presurgical suite, Jennifer Durante, who was head of communications at the Institute, and cameraman José Alkon, filmed a short interview. I admitted I was anxious about 'the craniotomy I'm having to remove, or debulk, as much of my tumour as possible without leaving too much functional deficit, but I know I'm in great hands with a great team of people. Fingers crossed it all goes well.'

I got an arterial line—a tube into an artery to allow constant measurement of my blood pressure. But before the operation, there was something I needed to discuss with Brindha, so the anaesthetist delayed giving me sedation.

We had agreed that after debulking the tumour, Brindha would use a syringe to squirt some immunotherapy drugs around the cavity that was left. But Georgina and Brindha had received an email overnight—shared with me—from the Belgian surgeon who had pioneered the intercranial administration of immunotherapy. He'd said he injected the drugs into the brain near the tumour as well as around the cavity. That raised the question of whether I should have this done, too.

When I raised it, Brindha said she hadn't injected drugs into the brain like that before and that there was no data to indicate it improved outcomes. We were both comfortable sticking with our original plan.

I was sedated.

Working in a theatre with an MRI scanner, Brindha progressively removed pieces of tumour, checked the scan then removed more. The operation took six hours.

Brindha and Georgina had spoken every day since I had been in Kraków. Having seen the stunning results that immunotherapy had had for patients with brain metastases from melanoma, she was 'on board 150 per cent' as soon as Georgina proposed the plan. While Brindha later admitted that her emotions had been all over the place treating a friend and considering what was safe for me, she always made me feel completely confident under her care.

While there was a view that immunotherapy would not work because of the so-called blood–brain barrier, a semi-permeable membrane between the blood vessels and the brain, we all knew this was not correct based on our melanoma data. Newer-generation targeted therapies and immunotherapy could get into the brain when there was a tumour.

When I woke up an hour after the operation, I was delighted to see Katie and Emily by my bed and I hugged them. Katie asked me some simple questions to test my awareness and memory. What year was it? Where was I? What was my name? Happily, I got 100 per cent. When she called by with Brindha, Georgina excitedly said, 'You didn't take the Richard out of Richard!'

I was elated to have got through the surgery without my brain function being impaired, and felt almost unbelievably well. I would get to enjoy more of my life before the tumour's likely recurrence.

In the intensive care unit later, my temperature kept spiking. The nursing staff were worried that, as a post-operative patient, I had an infection, so they followed a protocol that involved regularly taking blood, urine and stool samples, and a series of swabs. It was frustrating that I had to have all these things done when I believed, from having had a fever in recent days, that my temperature jumps were caused by the immunotherapy drugs rather than an infection. Even as a brain cancer patient, I couldn't forget that I was a doctor. The spiking eventually settled down.

Just before 7 p.m., I posted another update on X to say I was 'feeling great in the neuro ICU', and to thank Brindha, as well as friends and colleagues around the world who had been supporting me. I was appreciative when Brindha let me go home two days after surgery with a fresh scar and an intact mind.

DAY 30

While I waited for the pathology results, I had a day of being zonked out with medications then felt good again.

After special immunohistochemistry stains that used antibodies to check for certain antigens in the tumour tissue, neuropathologist Dr Laveniya Satgunaseelan called Georgina to tell her there were *so many* immune cells in the tumour taken after neoadjuvent immunotherapy, which suggested my immune system had been stimulated to act against the tumour.

Helen Rizos and her team also ran a lab test on single cells of the debulked tumour, called flow cytometry, which detected extra immune cells. In technical terms, she said they were white blood cells known as CD4 and CD8—so-called positive T cells—that could help attack cancer. And these additional immune cells were activated, which meant they were recognising and hopefully attacking the tumour cells.

Georgina excitedly told me there had been a tenfold increase in activated immune cells in the tumour taken in the debulking compared to the tissue taken in the biopsy before my first immunotherapy dose. Importantly, they were 'bound to drug', which meant Anti-PD-1 had penetrated into the tumour.

It was early days, but it was a phenomenal result. I hoped that it would increase the chance of my immune system killing the cancer cells in my residual tumour, though it was way too early to know.

DAY 34

Back at home, I posted a 'Day 6 post-op' video saying I felt pretty good in recovery and showing off my stitched-up incision scar. I mentioned the exciting news from the Institute's translational research team who had been looking at my specimens.

'There's some evidence on the immuno staining, and particularly through flow cytometry analysis, that there's activation of the immune system that wasn't there previously, which I guess fills me with some hope,' I said. 'We'll have to wait and see if this translates into clinical benefit but [it's] definitely an upside—[an] amazing thing to happen.'

I had been blown away by how generous and thoughtful people had been in response to my posts, particularly when I had been feeling low—tired, down on energy and anxious about the future. When I was feeling sorry for myself, that encouragement was good for my spirits.

Three days after the surgery, I felt even better and the scar looked less angry once the stitches had been taken out. I was getting my energy back, was sleeping better and was looking forward to getting out and about for the weekend, spending time with Katie and the kids.

DAY 38

As I recovered my strength, I felt happier than I had been for a while. I had come through the operation without losing brain function, and I was eager to be contributing to family life and work again. Katie and the kids continued to be amazingly supportive.

Like my dad, I had always loved family photos. So, in quiet moments, I went through some that we had taken on holidays. Thinking about these times made me happy. The kids looked so small when we were camping on the NSW south coast and bushwalking in Tasmania. I was so proud of who they had become. But it also struck me that I might not have many of these enjoyable family experiences ahead.

When I felt well enough, I slowly returned to exercising. As well as being something I loved to do, it helped my mental state. I set off for a long walk around the Bay Run track and back, and I felt well and truly smashed afterwards.

While surprised by how much fitness I'd lost, I had to remember I had gone through a six-hour operation. It would be best to keep my heart rate low-ish when I exercised for a while.

The next week, I felt strong enough to ride my bike to Haberfield to watch Matt race at Parkrun. He ran 5 kilometres in less than eighteen minutes—quicker than I'd run in the past decade. Probably quicker than I'd ever run.

DAY 43

I started having neurocognitive tests at the Institute—which I would have every eight weeks—to assess my attention, reaction time, processing speed, memory, language and cognition. The results would be compared over time to assess whether my brain function had changed during treatment.

I also had one of my regular lumbar punctures for clinical monitoring and research purposes. We wanted to see if there was a biomarker in my cerebrospinal fluid that would indicate the tumour had returned, or at least help with the difficult interpretation of radiology to detect early recurrence. Because radiology was sometimes inconclusive, we thought a biomarker could be another step in revolutionising brain cancer management.

It was not exactly an enjoyable procedure—curling into a ball on my side in a CT scanner for half an hour while cerebrospinal fluid was drawn from my spinal canal with a needle. Unfortunately, I ended up with headaches for a few days, probably because some of the fluid had leaked out of my spinal canal. But it was another way of using my illness to get data on glioblastoma. We wanted to do as much science during my treatment as possible. Switching between Wimbledon, the Ashes cricket series, the women's T20 cricket and the Tour de France on our new TV was a welcome distraction from these headaches.

DAY 46

I went back to working part-time in my offices at the Charles Perkins Centre and the Institute. People had asked why I wasn't just staying home and focusing on my treatment. The truth was that after almost three weeks recovering from the debulking operation, I wanted to both occupy my mind and continue contributing to melanoma research and treatment.

The kids were busy studying—Emily at uni, Matt in Year 12 and Lucy in Year 10. And while I had medical appointments with Katie just about every day, I felt I needed to engage with work instead of staying home and feeling sorry for myself.

Some people said I could still do my diagnostic work; others said I couldn't, presumably because there was doubt that I would be mentally sharp enough. While I felt as capable as ever, it would not be fair on my family if I went back to long hours diagnosing and reporting cases when I already had so many other commitments.

But working around my medical appointments, I began contributing again to research and resumed chairing the weekly multidisciplinary team meeting.

My second dose of combination immunotherapy was still on hold because of my abnormal liver-function tests. Hopefully it would settle soon.

Everything seemed promising so far, but there would be setbacks ahead.

9

AN OUTPOURING OF SUPPORT

Since going public with my diagnosis on social media, the Institute had been fielding media requests for interviews with me about what I was going through. I was happy to do whatever I could, because it was a chance to highlight our work and the importance of cancer research. Sometimes, though, I wondered: if I had limited time to live, was this what I wanted to put my energy into?

The first story that had an impact on everyone in my family was on the Nine Network's *A Current Affair*. It was promoted with a dramatic voiceover: 'The doctor gambling with his own life. One of the world's best cancer minds with the worst brain tumour. His death-defying treatment.'

This was certainly a different experience from other media interviews I'd done in the past about our work. I was usually talking about what our research at the Institute meant for the community, like when we released *State of the Nation— A Report into Melanoma* in 2022. Or I'd be explaining a breakthrough, like the Institute's calculators for melanoma risk and outcomes. Sometimes I'd be commenting on a public health issue, like the dangers of sunburn, the risks of tanning, the use of sunbeds or, in the case of our 'Game On Mole' campaign, the importance of seeing a healthcare professional if you observe something new or changing on your skin.

In those interviews, I had been an expert trying to make people aware of a pressing issue affecting Australians. To suddenly be the subject of the interview, as a patient struggling with a life-threatening cancer, was much more confronting.

While *A Current Affair* host Allison Langdon covered some of the science of my diagnosis and treatment, the story was largely about the emotion of what I was going through. 'I don't want to die,' I was filmed saying, near tears. 'I'm too young to die. I love my life. I really do.'

Ally noted there were eerie parallels in my story with that of my late friend and colleague Chris O'Brien—a doctor with incurable brain cancer who became the patient himself. 'Chris was a head and neck surgeon that I worked with then, all of a sudden, [he was] faced with this same brain cancer,' I said. 'It shocked me a bit. But ultimately everyone dies from it. No one gets cured, pretty much.'

Asked about the impact on my family, I said I thought I wasn't supporting Katie, especially, as much as I should be at times. But I explained how, even in this extreme situation where my life had been turned upside down by the glioblastoma diagnosis, I still wanted to have a crack at using science to beat brain cancer.

'It's scary what the future holds—to be now faced with certain death in a relatively short period of time,' I said. 'I'm not going to go down without keeping that drive going in trying to fight my own cancer. Hopefully a miracle happens.'

I watched the program with my family and, even though they'd known what to expect after seeing the promo, we were all close to tears. The kids hugged me afterwards. While there was nothing they didn't already know, having it summed up in the story seemed to bring it home to them.

I wondered how viewers would respond. I wasn't embarrassed about being so emotional; I was just doing what I'd been doing since I arrived back from Poland: being truthful about my prognosis, and my feelings of fear and hope. As it turned out, I was overwhelmed by positive feedback, love and encouragement from family, friends and colleagues that quickly expanded to acquaintances and people I had never met.

The story signalled a change: my personal fight was becoming a public one, which is what I had wanted. I had dedicated my life to helping people, in Australia and around the world. Sharing my story and talking about what I was learning was another way to do that.

Viewers, including other doctors, contacted me to say they hadn't felt comfortable going public about having cancer themselves but were impressed that I'd done it. I didn't have any privacy concerns, though. I was fine with being candid about what I was going through.

In a follow-up interview with Ray Hadley on Sydney radio station 2GB the next day, I pointed out that Australians had a one in two to one in three chance of getting skin cancer in their lifetime but just a one in 10,000 chance of getting a brain tumour. 'It's not such a common disease so it's harder to do research,' I said. 'And it's inside this hard box—the skull.'

Georgina, who was interviewed at the same time, compared my tumour to a fig tree, with a massive trunk and roots that were so extensive they could never be reached by surgery. 'You've got to use the immune system to keep the normal brain cells alive and try and utilise other ways to just selectively kill the cancer cells,' she said. The fig-tree analogy was a good one, and helped to explain that it was impossible to remove all of this type of tumour with surgery or radiotherapy.

Georgina said there were four outcomes for me with the experimental direction I'd taken: I could do worse than under standard treatment; I could do the same; I could do a little better; or there was 'a tiny chance' that I could be cured.

I saw it slightly differently: I could also stay alive for the same amount of time as with standard treatment, but have side effects from immunotherapy that would make my life awful. That was a lousy outcome. But it was true that I could do a little better, and there was a remote chance I could be cured. While sometimes I couldn't help thinking how shockingly cruel this disease was and how little time I probably had left with my family, I tried to stay optimistic.

Before the debulking operation, I had been anxious about whether I would survive it and what impact surgery would have on my brain. Afterwards, my anxiety shifted to whether the immunotherapy was going to work, how bad the side effects would be and when the tumour would return.

At the end of the 2GB interview, Ray generously called what I was doing 'one of the greatest acts of courage' he had ever seen. And while appreciating the compliment, I didn't see it like that. I had to try something that might save my life. After so many years of cancer research, why wouldn't I jump at the chance to blow open brain-tumour treatment? And, if the dreamed-of response happened, it might save my life.

Courage? I still felt like there was a cliff coming up—the tumour returning—and I didn't know when I was going to fall off it.

———

Since the start of treatment, I had been deep in discussions with my medical team, colleagues and Katie about how much radiotherapy I would have and where it would be directed to mop up some of the residual tumour.

The standard protocol for glioblastoma was six weeks of daily radiotherapy, Monday to Friday, at a dose of 60 gray (the measurement for joules of radiation per kilogram of matter) beginning three to four weeks after debulking. The dosage of radiotherapy and where it was directed could be adjusted.

As we had ditched the standard protocol, though, I weighed up the arguments carefully. Radiotherapy could cause radiation necrosis (the death of healthy tissue within the radiotherapy field), which might cause swelling and loss of function in the brain. Given the location of my tumour, that could be devastating. Radiotherapy could also have a delayed impact over one to two years, with seizures and loss of brain function likely long-term side effects.

There was a risk that it could affect my brain so much that there might come a time when we wouldn't know whether a seizure, or any other symptom I experienced, was a sign the tumour was back or a side effect of radiotherapy. The data for patients with glioblastoma didn't tell us much. Most people who had a lot of brain radiotherapy didn't survive long enough to have long-term effects. By aiming for a cure, I was hoping to be around in the long term, so I had to consider the risk of these side effects.

One of the reasons I was keen to have Michael Back as my radiation oncologist was his enthusiasm for precisely directing radiotherapy to the area that research showed the tumour would potentially spread to. Rather than it necessarily spreading in a circle, there were pathways that glioblastomas were more likely to take. Michael said that advances in radiological guidance meant that radiotherapy could be targeted much better than previously, and that he would be really strict about how far he would go into the 'normal' brain, particularly near critical areas like the brain stem. Under those circumstances, he lessened my concerns about side effects.

I took a calculated risk to go ahead with radiotherapy at the standard dose of 60 gray in the hope of mopping up as much of the residual tumour as possible.

Before it started, I needed to get a plastic mask made to go over my face and keep my head tightly in place during treatment. Because of where my tumour was, I knew the radiotherapy would go close to what's called the midbrain, which is crucial to functions that keep us alive and affect pretty much everything we do with our bodies, including movement, eating and even blinking. If the radiotherapy was even a millimetre off, it could have serious implications, so I didn't want to move my head even the slightest bit while having the treatments.

Many patients apparently feel claustrophobic when their masks are screwed down to the table. I was one of the unit's first to say 'tighter'. I figured the tighter, the better.

Radiotherapy—across the Harbour Bridge at Genesis-Care, St Leonards—turned out to be a simple process. It didn't hurt and took less than five minutes for each dose. I just relaxed during it; sometimes I'd almost fall asleep.

I felt my family were hopeful that things might tip in my favour, holding onto a small bit of hope that I'd be cured. They seemed proud that I was trying to be a part of changing brain cancer treatment, which helped me when

I felt low. It also helped when we did things together: going for walks, watching favourite TV shows and sometimes eating out at local restaurants.

Like work and family time, exercise was helping me deal with the anxiety around my treatment. In mid-July, I went for my first jog since the world championships in Spain in May, and felt good enough to start running regularly and riding on the indoor bike trainer.

It was concerning, though, that I was anaemic, with my haemoglobin level falling to less than 100 grams per litre (the norm for men is 130 to 180) at one stage. This could mean the immunotherapy was proving toxic to my bone marrow. Given my diet hadn't changed, another alarming possibility was that I was losing iron silently in bowel movements, something that was often caused by underlying bowel cancer.

When these possibilities were ruled out, it was concluded that the problem was how much blood I had been giving for both testing and laboratory research. It was sometimes up to 200 millilitres twice a week, which was equivalent to a weekly blood donation, and there wasn't enough iron in my blood to maintain adequate haemoglobin levels.

I started taking iron tablets and, when there was an opportunity in the coming weeks, had an iron transfusion. The team also reduced the volume of blood being taken for both standard toxicity monitoring and research.

After further liver-function tests, I had my third dose of immunotherapy—just Anti-PD-1 and Anti-LAG-3 this time, because Anti-CTLA-4 was the most likely of the three drugs to be affecting my liver.

I finished radiotherapy in late August, and it was remarkable how smoothly it had gone, with little of the extra fatigue that was expected or any neurocognitive changes. In fact, the biggest challenge turned out to be getting to St Leonards every day, given I wasn't allowed to drive because I'd had seizures within the previous twelve months. Katie would usually drive me—yet another thing I was grateful to her for since that first seizure in Poland.

I felt so good on the morning before the last radiotherapy dose that I went for a 12-kilometre jog.

———

Then there was a setback.

After riding on the indoor trainer in the early morning a few days after my last radiotherapy dose, I had another seizure and passed out. Katie, who came into the room after I collapsed, called an ambulance and I was taken to emergency at RPA.

An MRI scan didn't reveal anything worrying, so I went home. Helen Wheeler, my neuro-oncologist, started me on a new anti-epileptic drug because of the full-on seizure and what the experts called partial seizures—up to five a day—that I'd been having. On anti-seizure medication, people usually don't have full seizures but, with these so-called partial ones, I would feel cold peripherally—in my fingers and toes—have a funny taste in my mouth and experience a wave of nausea. Then it would pass in a minute or two, and I would feel normal again.

With the new anti-seizure medication, Helen said that if I had another full-on seizure, there would be no need to go to hospital. She would simply adjust my medications again.

Radiotherapy reputedly makes patients feel tired after it finishes. I wasn't sure if it was that, or the new anti-epileptic drug I was on, but after my last radiotherapy session I had the toughest week of my treatment so far. I felt worn out, lethargic and irritable.

One Saturday morning around this time, I was cheered up by a science fiction–looking photo of me in my lab coat and goggles, taken by Tim Bauer, on the cover of *The Sydney Morning Herald* and *The Age*'s *Good Weekend* magazine. While it was a thrill being profiled for the magazine, I was also nervous about reading it. What had I said and how had it been interpreted? What had other people said about me? What would readers think?

Georgina declared her optimism for my treatment in the story: 'Usually, as doctors, we're not allowed to hope. Using the word "cure" is almost seen as childish because, like, what if it doesn't work? But now, with Richard, we're going for a cure. That's the blue sky, the ultimate goal.'

It was a good story but I regretted that it didn't show how grateful I was to the kids for all their support. I couldn't have asked for the whole family to be more caring. My diagnosis meant we'd been expressing our love for each other more openly than before.

But, unfortunately, I had also been more irritable at times than I used to be, and, of course, my family felt the effects. I thought that could be down to one (or more) of several factors: the emotion of having cancer, the location of the tumour in the emotional-regulation part of my brain, the side effects of my medications, not getting enough sleep and having less autonomy in my life.

It could have been a lot tougher, though. When I had started immunotherapy, my side effects had been most prominent after the first dose, with fevers that made it hard to sleep, nausea, vomiting, uncontrollable shivers and some gastrointestinal symptoms. The worst side effects after that had been a rash and abnormal liver-function tests.

For many patients, it was much more brutal.

Sometimes immunotherapy could result in immune cells attacking the pancreas, which meant a patient could get diabetes. If it attacked liver or thyroid cells, it could result in liver or thyroid failure. If it attacked the gut cells, it might cause diarrhoea. Some patients found immunotherapy affected their gut so badly that their large intestine had to be removed, which might mean having to use a colostomy bag. Sometimes—very rarely—a patient's melanoma would be cured but they would die from the immunotherapy's side effects.

About 60 per cent of people who had *two* immuno-therapy drugs had 'major adverse events', so I was grateful I hadn't had anything really significant with *three* drugs. Various theories had been suggested about why this was the case, including how much exercise I had been doing during treatment. To me, it seemed most likely to be my inherited genetics. I was just lucky. While I went on to have what's called grade 3 liver toxicity, a major factor in me getting through without more serious issues was the excellent management of immunotherapy at the Institute.

Whether it was a result of immunotherapy or radio-therapy, my anti-epileptic medications needed to be increased and changed over the coming months to control the partial seizures, which had increased to many times a day. I kept quiet about them but they'd become distressingly frequent.

While I was going well physically other than that, Katie sometimes thought I wasn't faring so well emotionally and was pushing myself too hard when it came to exercise. The first part was true—I definitely struggled at times. I wasn't sure about the second, though. Maybe I was driving myself too hard, but exercise gave me a lot of pleasure and lifted my mood, which were important for helping me deal with anxiety and stay as optimistic as possible. I also wanted to enjoy the limited time I might have left and a run at sunrise was one way of doing that.

———

For everyone in the family, my diagnosis had turned life upside down. When we first met Helen Wheeler, she said cancer was often tougher on the patient's partner than on the patient because they might not get the same attention and care. 'Make sure Katie gets support, too, because it is going to be a tough road for both of you,' she said.

Katie had been incredibly generous to me and our family for a long time. I had been so driven at work, and my additional responsibilities at the Institute, including having to travel more, had kept me away from home. I'd been selfish at times, which made it hard for everyone. Now I felt terrible about dumping cancer on her, with all the increased stresses and responsibilities it brought, and the uncertainties and potential risks of the treatment I was undertaking.

As difficult as it was, we talked about what life would be like when I was gone—how she'd cope being on her own, how she'd look after the kids, how she'd manage financially. In the past we'd talked about touring around Australia and going camping when we retired. It didn't seem like that would happen now, which was deeply sad.

It was hard to know how much the kids had been shaken up. But as well as being more open about expressing our love with hugs and kisses, we'd had long talks about all sorts of topics, including what was happening in their everyday lives, what made them happy, what they might do for work in the future, where they wanted to travel and their deeper feelings about my brain cancer.

I felt it wouldn't be right for them to put their lives on hold and wait around for Dad to cark it. So I made sure we did fun activities together, like tenpin bowling, playing basketball and going to the cinema. I wanted them to enjoy their lives and make the most of the opportunities they had in front of them.

Every so often, I'd forget what I was going through. If someone was talking about racing a triathlon in Hawaii or having a holiday in South America, I'd think, 'I'd love to do that.' Then I'd remember why I couldn't. 'Shit,' I'd think. 'The odds of me being able to do something like that in a year's time are not very good.'

Sometimes I was asked whether I felt like I had to make the most of every day since my diagnosis. That was when I realised I hadn't gone very far through the stages of grief. I presume many people who get a terminal diagnosis will accept, after a time, that their outcome is determined. But I didn't feel I'd reached that point. I wasn't going down without a fight.

Even a year after that seizure in Poland, I still hadn't accepted it. I was still fighting.

With all this going on, I found a lot to talk about with the cancer psychologists lined up for me at Lifehouse and Royal North Shore Hospital. They thought I was heading down the right path with how I was coping emotionally. But I definitely had bad days as well as good days.

Probably every day I thought about how little time I might have left. Sometimes I felt other people, even those closest to me, had trouble really 'getting' how emotional that made me feel—the anxiety and the fear about what was ahead. I guess it is something you have to go through yourself to fully understand.

I did a lot of talking about cancer in a ton of media interviews that followed the *Good Weekend* story. There were stories with *The Australian*, ABC Radio National, Sky News Australia, Radio New Zealand, Australian Associated Press, ABC Radio Sydney and *Bloomberg News*. This last article quoted three leading cancer researchers from American universities who were watching what we were trying. Roger Stupp, who had pioneered the Stupp protocol, agreed with our decision to skip chemotherapy, saying, 'You cannot win a Formula 1 race with one foot on the gas pedal, and the other on the brakes.'

My treatment entered a new phase when Maria Gonzalez, the Institute's head of clinical trials, gave me my first personalised cancer-vaccine shot. People asked, 'Is this to prevent all cancers?' No, it was designed specifically for my tumour. It was trying to enhance my immune system to recognise the glioblastoma and fight it.

A bigger volume of vaccine was injected than for a normal flu or COVID shot. My arm hurt a lot more than I expected for days, and this pain continued for the next few doses, but luckily I didn't develop the flu-like illness that affected some patients. By the second week of September 2023, my energy levels had picked up and Georgina was fine with me having my fourth dose of immunotherapy—just Anti-CTLA-4 this time, to assess its impact on my liver-function tests.

Amid all the public interest in my treatment, Georgina and I spoke for the second time at the National Press Club, exactly a year to the day since our first speech. Instead of going to Canberra, the venue this time was the Kerry Packer Education Centre Packer at RPA. Like our first speech, it would be televised live around the country.

Adding to the emotion of another raw and candid speech was that Katie, Matt and Lucy were sitting in the front row. The audience also included my brother Mark and his partner Anna, Katie's family, Georgina's family, federal education minister Jason Clare—a former melanoma patient and co-chair of the Parliamentary Friends of Melanoma and Skin Cancer Awareness group—and many of our medical and university colleagues. Among them were Jim Finlay, James Groom and former Tasmanian premier Will Hodgman.

While our previous speech was to put melanoma prevention in the national spotlight, we had a broader agenda this time. Inspired by the scientific breakthroughs we'd made in the last ten weeks, we called on the global cancer treatment community to think big, be courageous and challenge the conventional paradigm by looking beyond just one cancer, particularly for patients who were dying on standard treatments. We want to push for better clinical trials that ensured more access for patients, and more research that was embedded into clinical care to generate scientific data faster.

Georgina had an evocative phrase that explained immunotherapy: it was like 'sniffer dogs being trained through exposure to illicit drugs so when they get to work, they know what they are searching for'.

Detailing the emotional time since my seizure in Poland, I said, 'I've cried, we've cried as a family—we still do,' and I described myself as the first patient in what might become the new frontier for brain cancer treatment. 'In addition to the novel treatments I'm having, I've also chosen to have additional tests and procedures, purely for research,' I said. 'This includes a riskier open biopsy, delayed resection of my tumour, multiple lumbar punctures, multiple scans and blood tests, and various other cognitive tests.

'Science has a long history of being pushed forward by scientists [using] themselves as subjects. What I'm doing may not be as extreme as the likes of Marie and Pierre Curie, who routinely exposed themselves to radiation and suffered the consequences for the rest of their lives. But hopefully the scientific learnings we will generate will be just as profound.'

Georgina detailed the pushbacks we had faced, including the widely held view that brain cancer was immuno-suppressive so it wouldn't respond to immunotherapy, and that it was heterogeneous—full of different cancer cells—so it would be impossible to target all of them effectively.

'These were not barriers for us,' she said. 'We had navigated all of these supposed barriers in melanoma itself, including using immunotherapy to treat tumours which had spread to the brain. We were comfortable [enough] as cancer researchers to not have fear.'

Georgina added that the promising early scientific findings, including a tenfold increase in immune cells within the tumour, meant 'some forward-thinking biopharma-ceutical companies are investigating starting programs for glioblastoma'.

Our call to bolster clinical trials to develop more life-saving treatments was based on the fact that fewer than 6 per cent of all cancer patients were on a clinical trial in Australia in 2022—a bleak state of affairs for patients with the most difficult-to-treat cancers, who had to settle for standard treatments even when they were, like mine, incurable. 'Pharmaceutical companies need to invest and open clever clinical trials that include *all* cancers, even rare cancers,' I said.

Georgina continued: 'Drug companies should consider the 50,000 people dying from cancer in Australia, not just, for example, the 1300 dying from glioblastoma. Then they can generate monumental change.'

We hoped the speech would create waves in cancer treatment around the world. For the moment, as we mingled with guests after the session, it seemed to be well received. While Katie and the kids seemed proud that I was doing something that would help other people, I suspect they also felt sad about the very public reminder that my brain cancer was incurable.

The next day I had my second personalised vaccine—my arm really hurt again—then, four days later, my fifth dose of immunotherapy. It was Anti-PD-1 and Anti-LAG-3 this time.

There was a surprise soon afterwards when Matthew Browne, the chief executive of the Institute, told Georgina and me that the NSW premier's office wanted to speak to us. When we called, we learned we were finalists for the NSW Australian of the Year for what they described as an 'enduring partnership' that had 'saved thousands of lives from melanoma', and developing trailblazing treatments based on our melanoma breakthroughs to treat my brain cancer.

What an honour!

I wasn't sure it was going to be possible but I was given the green light from my medical team to head to Chicago to accept another notable honour: the Founders' Award from the American Society of Dermatopathology, to be presented at their annual meeting. Katie stayed at home because Matt had Higher School Certificate exams very soon. My brother Mark joined me on the journey, which I was nervous about making, concerned about the health problems I might have while I was away. It was my first trip overseas since my cancer diagnosis and my first time overseas with Mark since we'd been to South Africa as kids.

Before heading to the airport, I had another dose of immunotherapy—just Anti-CTLA-4. On the way, Mark and I reminisced about our time in South Africa. I really enjoyed spending so much time with him again.

In Chicago, I felt honoured to get a standing ovation when I collected an award that was rarely given to anyone from outside North America. Mark and I packed a lot into two and a half days on the ground. We went for a run with my long-time American friend and collaborator Klaus Busam on the triathlon course where I had raced at the 2015 World Triathlon championships, and I caught up with long-time medical friends, including Jeff Gershenwald and Pedram Gerami. Just as he was when we were growing up, Mark was a very caring brother throughout the trip. Being so friendly, he was a hit with my American colleagues at social events.

Right before leaving Chicago, I felt a little unwell with pre-seizure–like symptoms. I took extra anti-epileptic tablets and thankfully made it home without incident.

Katie was able to join me for another quick international trip soon afterwards, where I presented a talk on how we were using our melanoma discoveries for my glioblastoma treatment and I received the Lifetime Achievement Award at the International Congress of the Society for Melanoma Research in Philadelphia. I was touched to get another standing ovation.

Arriving back in Sydney, I went virtually straight from the airport to a morning tea at Government House, where I met the other finalists for NSW Australian of the Year. They all seemed so deserving of the recognition: social worker and Muslim Women Australia chief executive Maha Abdo, engineer and clean-energy advocate Dr Saul Griffith, and mental fitness advocate and Gotcha4Life Foundation founder Gus Worland. We also met the finalists in the other three categories: NSW Local Hero, Young Australian and Senior Australian of the Year.

We thought we had no chance.

When Premier Chris Minns read out our names as winners at the Museum of Contemporary Art that night, Georgina and I were as stunned as we were thrilled. Everyone had been asked to prepare an acceptance speech in case they won and we had decided to outline the extent of the melanoma public health crisis—one Australian was diagnosed every 30 minutes, one died every six hours, and it was the most common cancer for 20-to-39-year-olds in our country. We also said how grateful we were to our families for their backing.

Later we realised that this award gave us a platform to push for changes that would help more Australians. While our melanoma work, for all its success, had never been particularly high profile, my brain cancer and the bold treatment we were trying based on our melanoma discoveries had struck a chord.

———————

When it came time for my first MRI scan in two months, I wasn't feeling overly anxious because it seemed too early for the tumour to come back and I hadn't had any worrying symptoms. I was right: it was clear. I felt elated and relieved.

The latest clinical trial data said median survival for my brain tumour's subtype was about fourteen months, with median recurrence in six months. These scans now took me to six months, so I was past the median time for recurrence.

Then there was a worrying incident.

In November, I passed out with another seizure at home. I was sitting at the dining table and speaking on the phone when it hit. Lucy, my youngest daughter, called an ambulance but when I came round, I told them we didn't need them. Helen Wheeler made another adjustment to my anti-epileptic medications so hopefully it wouldn't happen again. While going unconscious was rare, I was still having many partial seizures.

Since the trip to Poland, my weight had dropped from 82 to 76 kilograms. My medications often made me feel sick so I didn't feel like eating as much as normal. My family and close friends were often urging me to eat more.

Even this far into my treatment, I had a medical appointment most days. I relied on my highly efficient, dedicated and kind executive assistant, Kara Taylor, to help me juggle all these appointments, along with work commitments and more media interviews.

For a while, I had been filmed for an episode of the ABC's *Australian Story* that was taking a close look at what I was going through. When it screened, it was another emotional story that featured scenes of my family in Sydney, my parents and Mark in Tassie, my doctors and my treatment. Emily was impressive when asked about what we were going through as a family. She said my diagnosis had been a shock, but remembered how immediately there had been discussions about what we were going to do about it and how we were going to move forward with treatment. While it would have been really easy for me to stop doing everything that had made me who I was and just worry about the cancer, Emily noted that I hadn't slowed down since I'd been diagnosed.

There were many tears when we watched the show together as a family. Then came another outpouring of public support that I could not have imagined earlier in the year. The kindness of people—their warm encouragement— lifted my spirits. People were stopping me in the street to say 'Good luck with your treatment', and making other generous comments.

There was one moment, though, when I realised I needed to watch what I did and said in public. Soon after *Australian Story*, Georgina and I flew to Canberra to speak about putting sun safety in sport on the national agenda. With our flight running behind time and a delay collecting luggage, it looked like we would be late for our presentation at the Australian Institute of Sport. As we joined a long taxi queue, I called out, 'Anyone know where the Uber pick-up is?' Two ladies turned around and pointed it out. 'You guys were so good on *Australian Story*,' one of them said. When the taxi line started moving, we stayed in it and had a conversation with her about my treatment. It was clear that a lot of people had watched the show.

That was also evident when I went to Launceston with Emily, Matt and Lucy for an early Christmas lunch with Mum and Dad. Mark and his kids, Noah and Maia, flew in from Melbourne for the weekend, too. My friend Jim, who put us up at his place, had organised a cycle on Sunday morning to welcome me back to Tassie.

With all the interest generated by *Australian Story*, the group included two Launceston sporting stars: legendary cyclist Richie Porte, the former Tour de France third-placegetter who was still super fit after retiring, and triathlete Jake Birtwhistle, a gold, silver and bronze medal-list at the Commonwealth Games. I was impressed by how down to earth and modest they both were and their interest in what I was going through as we spoke on the ride and at a coffee shop in town afterwards. *The Examiner*, the Launceston paper, had a photo of the ride on page one the next day, noting that both Richie and I were originally Riverside boys.

Dad was still living at Legana but Mum was in a nursing home. There was a competition at the home for who had the best Christmas decorations so the grandkids dressed up her room. Then I brought Mum to Dad's place in a taxi and we all had a really enjoyable early Christmas lunch together before going through some of Dad's photo albums.

Before Christmas Day, there was another trip to Canberra. As NSW Australians of the Year, Georgina and I were finalists for the 2024 Australian of the Year. Our first commitment was attending the launch of an exhibition at the National Museum of Australia, built on the site of the old Canberra Hospital where I had spent time as a medical student.

The other contenders were an inspirational group: Build Like A Girl founder Joanne Farrell (representing the ACT), Central Australian Youth Link-Up Service founder Blair McFarland (Northern Territory), Indigenous health leader Janine Mohamed (Victoria), Men of Business founder Marco Renai (Queensland), rural women's advocate and Motherland founder Stephanie Trethewey (Tasmania), environmental scientist and advocate Tim Jarvis (South Australia), and advocate for victims of crime Mechelle Turvey (Western Australia).

Every nominee had been invited to send a significant item that would be exhibited at the museum. Not sure what they wanted, Georgina and I sent a heap of gear, including a copy of WHO *Classification of Skin Tumours*, which I had co-edited. They selected my Australian race suit from the 2019 World Triathlon championships in Lausanne.

Georgina, who is also a triathlete, had competed at the same world championships, so they chose her race medal.

For us, these items represented the importance of participating in health and fitness in a sun-safe way, as well as the teamwork, collaboration and participation that were as vital in medical research as they were in sport. It was a chance to spread the message that we trained early in the morning or in the evenings and, if we were ever outside during the day, we wore sun-protective clothing and used sunblock on any exposed skin.

Georgina also made the point, when we were interviewed on stage, that triathlon was a sport that could fit into a busy schedule. 'You could train in your own time,' she said. 'I'm the opposite to Richard. Richard is an early bird; I'm a late owl.'

I noted that, like competing in triathlon, our work at the Institute was on the world stage. 'Australia has the highest incidence of melanoma anywhere in the world, and we've led very important discoveries in the science and treatment of melanoma that have resulted in incredible changes,' I said. 'Georgina brought up prevention as well. That's also very important for us.

'We know Australia is an iconic sports nation . . . We all love our sport. Prevention of melanoma in sport is something we need to address a lot more at all levels, from grassroots level up to elite level . . . to try and improve long-term outlooks for participants, spectators and even officials. We want to get that message out to the Australian public:

the importance of prevention in melanoma [and] sun-smart behaviour in sport.'

When we had received our Australian outfits for those Lausanne world championships, I thought it wasn't right that they only had a singlet-style top. It would be much more sun-safe to have a suit that covered competitors' backs, shoulders and upper arms. Triathlon Australia approached the world governing body and requested one but were knocked back.

After the race, Triathlon Australia made a formal submission to the governing body, which was accepted. It became possible to wear a suit that covered more of your upper body, which was especially important when you were riding the bike. It was a small change but another step towards reducing the risk of skin cancer in sport.

———

We had been having a short family holiday at Culburra on the NSW south coast and had planned to extend it after our time in Canberra but a sad event took us back to Sydney. My mentor, Stan McCarthy, had died.

I had visited him in a nursing home not long before I went to Poland. Stan had Parkinson's disease and had been going downhill. While I wasn't sure he'd recognise me, I was really pleased that he did, and we spent a warm couple of hours reminiscing about our time together.

In my speech at his funeral, I described Stan as a remarkable man, a brilliant yet humble pathologist who changed the lives of hundreds of thousands of Australians with his expert diagnosis, contributions to research and mentoring of generations of pathologists. 'I feel incredibly privileged to have had Stan as a great friend and also to have worked in partnership with him in diagnosis and research,' I said.

I meant every word. He did so much for me, and meant so much to me.

I'd always thought of myself as an emotional person, but now milestones like Stan's death were making me more emotional than ever. Another significant one was my 57th birthday in December, given I might not have a 58th. Katie organised a fantastic lunch at a restaurant overlooking Sydney Harbour, and the family laughed a lot as we remembered holidays and other fun times we'd shared.

I was even more emotional on Christmas Day. The morning started with a Parkrun; I managed a solid 20 minutes, 14 seconds for the 5 kilometres. Then, before a Christmas lunch that Katie and the kids had organised for sixteen relatives and friends at our place, I was filming an update for social media when I was suddenly overwhelmed by the poignancy of the day.

'Given the prognosis for the sort of brain cancer that I've got, the odds of me being around for next year's [celebration] is not high,' I said. 'If I follow the average, this will be my last Christmas with friends and relatives. I sincerely hope that's not the case but it's certainly drawn the emotions out of me.'

Everyone enjoyed the Christmas lunch and I later saw, from the warm-hearted comments and messages on social media, that there were many people on my side. Their kindness lifted my spirits.

Early in the new year, I struggled with a heavy cold that worsened after my tenth dose of immunotherapy and meant I wasn't able to enjoy the holidays or exercise much. It turned out to have been caused by autoimmune sinusitis, which was complicated by an infection. But there were a couple of bright moments amid the gloom.

The first was celebrating Lucy's sixteenth birthday. Our youngest child was sixteen! Then the Australian cricket captain Pat Cummins visited to interview me for a book he was writing on leadership. He had been an exceptional leader since taking over the Test team and, in person, I was impressed by how refreshingly intelligent, articulate and down to earth he was. Matt is a huge cricket fan so I was thrilled that he got to meet Pat as well.

As the months had progressed, I had grown more nervous about my regular MRI scans. The more time that passed, the more likely it was that the tumour would be back. I had a scan in December and, happily, there was no sign that the tumour had returned. I was out to eight months without recurrence!

Next, the family was headed to Canberra for the announcement of the 2024 Australian of the Year. It was unlikely we'd win but who knew?

10

AUSTRALIAN OF
THE YEAR

Taking the bike was a last-minute decision. After a restless night, I had slept in and was late for our local Parkrun. I saw Matt jogging out the door and knew he'd be too far ahead to catch up with by the time I was ready, so I jumped on my bike.

I was riding on the Parramatta Road footpath, heading quickly down Taverners Hill, when—*bam!*—I hit a bump. In what felt like slow motion, I went over the handlebars and landed heavily on my head. *Ohhh no!* I was sliding. *This is bad!* I stopped and saw my bike cartwheeling across two lanes into the traffic. *Body hurts*. I was dazed.

Picking myself up, I worked out what damage I'd done. I was wearing a helmet so my head was okay. I felt grazes on my face, legs, hands, elbows and right shoulder. I was alive.

But not in great shape. I dragged my bike off the road, where it had been holding up the traffic.

In shock, I sat down against a fence beside the footpath and caught my breath. A few minutes later, a friendly kid and his dad arrived with a first aid kit. I said something like 'Thanks, I'm fine'—but I wasn't sure I was. I got back on the bike, gingerly. My kind helpers looked concerned. I said 'Thanks' again. The dad told me to take it carefully.

I rode to the Greenway Parkrun at Haberfield but I had missed the start of the race. I chained up my bike and, still recovering, started jogging to catch the walkers at the tail end of the field. My mouth was dry. I could see blood on the back of my hands. I touched my cheek. More blood.

I saw people I knew, including Matt, heading back in the opposite direction to the finish while I was still running to the turnaround. When they were close, I saw some of them mouth 'hello' then reel at what I looked like.

It was Saturday, 20 January. Any day was a bad day to have a bike crash, especially going down Taverners Hill at more than 30 kilometres an hour; especially when you were a supposedly responsible doctor, medical leader, husband and father; especially when you were going through revolutionary brain cancer treatment.

But this was an *especially* bad day because, in three days, I was due to head to Canberra with Katie and the kids for the announcement of the 2024 Australian of the Year.

I'd been sent a schedule with a packed program of events to attend before Prime Minister Anthony Albanese announced the Local Hero, Junior Australian, Senior Australian and Australian of the Year on Thursday night. Lots of meeting famous people, lots of mingling, probably lots of explaining about my brain cancer and my treatment.

Taking it v-e-r-y-y-y-y steadily, I ran 5 kilometres in 27 minutes flat. Even banged up, I couldn't help feeling competitive. I was disappointed by my time, but I made it, which hadn't seemed likely when I'd gone over the handlebars.

I chatted with Matt at the finish. He'd had a strong run but was worried when he saw the blood on my cheek and limbs. 'What happened?' he said. 'Are you okay?' I told him about hitting the bump.

Walking the bike home with Matt, I could feel a depression in my cheekbone and feared it was broken. I knew I'd have to go to emergency at RPA. Back home, Katie wanted to get me there as soon as possible. I called a head and neck surgeon friend from the Institute, Kerwin Shannon, who let his colleagues know I was heading in.

With Katie waiting patiently at the hospital, I spent the afternoon getting scans, then dressings on all my grazes. I was upset with myself. It was stupid riding like that. Why hadn't I stuck my phone into my shorts instead of holding it in one hand as I gripped the handlebars?

The radiology scans showed my cheekbone wasn't broken. There was also no bleeding in my brain. But radiologist Elizabeth Thompson, a friend, showed me a scan and told me I had a vertical fracture in the C6 vertebral body in my neck. Wow—a broken neck! Both Katie and I were stunned.

I could have become a quadriplegic. *I just did the Parkrun with a broken neck!*

I had more X-rays as I flexed and extended my neck. They showed the break was not expanding, which meant the ligaments around the joint hadn't been ruptured. It was what's called a stable fracture, meaning the two sides of the bone are still in the same place. I didn't need an operation and there was no risk of damage to my spinal cord from the bone moving. I could still go to Canberra for the big announcement. I headed home wearing a neck brace and rested.

On Monday, Katie and I saw Brindha at Lifehouse. Despite her usual calm and sympathetic manner, she was clearly exasperated. (Perhaps neurosurgeons are not used to their brain cancer patients complicating their treatment with bike crashes.) She was already concerned that I'd been pushing myself too hard and exercising too much. I'd been lucky, she said. Thankfully, she was fine with me going to Canberra, and, because the fracture was stable, I didn't need to wear the neck brace.

When I told Georgina about the fracture, she was shocked, but relieved the damage wasn't more serious.

I spent the rest of the day with the family—everyone was sympathetic and looked after me. Luckily, we had already bought some new clothes that were suitable for the week ahead so I didn't need to go shopping before we left.

I talked to Jen Durante, who handled communications for the Institute, and we decided to keep the broken neck quiet outside family and close friends. It would be a distraction during the media interviews that were being lined up for Georgina and me in Canberra. We wanted to use the opportunity to stress the importance of sun safety and the dangers of tanning.

———————

Katie and I flew to Canberra on Tuesday, and headed to the Crowne Plaza, which was the headquarters for the Australian of the Year Awards. I was self-conscious about my various grazes and my neck was a little sore but I could pass for healthy. Most people were too polite to ask about the graze on my cheek. I suspect that many would have thought it was related to my cancer treatment.

Seeing how the hotel had been decked out reminded Katie and me that this week was a big deal. There was an Australian of the Year desk in the foyer, with enthusiastic staff to answer questions and steer nominees and their families to a fleet of shuttle buses that would take us to events. There were pictures of the nominees on the front desk and lift doors.

The most special feature, though, were the portraits of past Australians of the Year that were hanging over four storeys in the hotel atrium—tremendous people like Sir Edward 'Weary' Dunlop (1976), Paul Hogan (1985), Fred Hollows (1990), Cathy Freeman (1998), Pat Rafter (2002), Steve Waugh (2004), Dr Fiona Wood (2005) and Adam Goodes (2014), alongside more recent winners Grace Tame (2021), Dylan Alcott (2022) and Taryn Brumfitt (2023).

Wow, wow, wow! Katie and I were awestruck. They were all remarkable Australians but I was especially pleased to see scientists Ian Frazer (2006) and Sir Gustav Nossal (2000), as well as some of the sports stars I'd loved watching compete.

All the events were brilliantly organised by the National Australia Day Council, and everyone was so generous to us. Originally, we only had three tickets to events—one for Katie, one for me and one for whoever else we wanted to bring. When the organisers found out that we (and other nominees) had more than one kid, they said we could bring them all.

The kids came to Canberra separately because of their different commitments—Matt drove our car, Emily caught the train and Lucy caught the bus—and it was fantastic to see them when they arrived, buzzing about what was ahead and excited to go to events at the Australian War Memorial and the governor-general's residence at Government House, and to the big announcement at the National Arboretum, overlooking Molonglo Valley. Georgina was excited to have her husband Greg and her daughters Livia, Lucia and Ella joining us for the week as well.

After some filming for the Australia Day Council, there was a finalists-only event at the National Museum of Australia, where the Australian of the Year exhibition was running. We had met most of the other nominees at the exhibition launch before Christmas, but this was a chance to learn more about their inspiring lives and contributions to society before we headed to a dinner for nominees and their families. I forgot about my broken neck amid all the excitement.

Functions at night were tricky for me. With a recently increased dosage of one anti-epileptic medication as well as a new one to get my partial seizures more under control—both of which had a sedative effect—I'd been heading to bed early. Before dessert, Katie escorted me back to the hotel in an Uber so I could sleep.

———

Lunches for the four Australian of the Year categories, at four venues around the city, were planned for the following day. Ours was at the swanky Boat House restaurant by Lake Burley Griffin, where I remembered going with the late Professor Peter Herdson, Jane Dahlstrom, Paul Whiting and other colleagues as a registrar at Canberra Hospital. It reminded me what a top mentor he'd been, how much I'd liked living in Canberra and how much had happened since then.

At the lunch, I enjoyed talking to Marco Renai, who had raised $1 million to build a senior high school for at-risk young men in Queensland, and Stephanie Trethewey, who had set up the Motherland support network for rural mothers around Australia from her home in Tasmania. I learned that one of her husband's best friends was a former pathology fellow, Dr Louise Jackett, who I'd trained, mentored and supervised for her PhD. While it is not quite true that all Tasmanians know each other, we were very proud to be from there.

Afterwards, there was a late-afternoon function at the War Memorial, a museum I knew well from many visits over the years. Back on the bus, we swung by Old Parliament House for a special moment: we had our photos taken beside flags that carried our portraits. The Australia Day Council had gone to so much trouble to make the awards feel important for all of the nominees.

Then we headed to a reception at Government House. As soon as we got off the bus, I could see what a stunning event it was. After being greeted with an Aboriginal smoking ceremony, we walked onto an immaculate green lawn leading down to Lake Burley Griffin, with a marquee and dozens of waiters handing around finger food and drinks.

On that warm sunny evening, we found ourselves talking to all sorts of people—many of them recognised in the Australia Day honours list—while our kids mingled with Georgina's and Marco's kids. I was impressed with how grown-up Emily, Matt and Lucy looked in their formal outfits. Katie was stunning in a stylish dress, and had a warm smile and conversation for everyone we met.

When I had worked at Canberra Hospital, I'd lived near Government House, in a little townhouse next to the brick-works. I'd ridden bikes, jogged and competed in triathlons around the lake. But I'd never been inside the grounds of the governor-general's residence before and, as the sun sank and the lake shimmered, I saw how magnificent a setting it was for an event. I was thrilled that Katie and the kids could share in an experience like this.

I met more of the nominees from other categories, their extremely proud families and previous winners. I hit it off with Nikhil Autar, a young doctor who had just started working at Sydney's Royal North Shore Hospital and was the NSW Young Australian of the Year. Diagnosed with leukaemia at seventeen, he had gone through chemotherapy, bone-marrow transplants and open heart surgery, and was in a wheelchair much of the time. But, as well as studying medicine, he had founded a social enterprise that supplied low-cost medical devices for people in need. Nikhil had also developed a device that allowed ordinary beds to be converted into hospital beds, and created maps to guide people with disabilities on visits to major Sydney hospitals, universities, restaurants and other public places. He was also, I found, a very likeable guy who had achieved amazing things despite all the adversity he had experienced.

I also enjoyed meeting the Northern Territory Young Australian of the Year, Peter Susanto, who was a medical student. He had come third when he represented the country in the International Brain Bee Olympiad, a competition centred on the brain and neuroscience. He was another young achiever who deserved the recognition.

Under a marquee, Governor-General David Hurley made a heartfelt speech about the importance of the awards. It was such a relaxed event that a young boy was rolling on the grass in front of the stage during the speech. Afterwards, the governor-general's wife, Linda Hurley, led everyone in singing the old song 'You Are My Sunshine'. After a rousing first verse, she asked everyone to turn to the next person and sing the second verse to them. I'm not the best singer but everyone was joining in, so I did my best. I later learned she did this at events all the time, I guess as a way of bringing people together.

When the effects of the increased anti-epileptics kicked in, Katie could see I was struggling. There were buses that would take the kids later, so Kate and I caught an Uber back to the hotel before the reception finished.

While Georgina and I doubted we would win Australian of the Year, because the other contenders were so inspiring, all the nominees had to prepare a three-minute speech in case they won. Because there were two of us, Georgina and I had been given six minutes to say what we'd like to achieve with the award.

We were supposed to have submitted a final version the previous Friday but we hadn't finished it. The bike crash had meant I was at RPA for much of Saturday, then worse for wear on Sunday. Georgina saw her melanoma patients on Mondays, so we had worked on the speech at the airport on the way to Canberra, then in the little spare time we'd had since. Now here we were, on the night before the big event, and our speech was still unfinished.

It was the day of the ceremony, Thursday, 25 January. Katie, Georgina, Greg and I headed to a morning tea hosted by Prime Minister Anthony Albanese and his partner (later fiancé) Jodie Haydon for all the nominees at The Lodge, his official residence. I remember, years ago, looking down the driveway while running past, so it was a thrill—in a week full of them—to go inside. On a lawn in a beautiful garden, it was a much more intimate function than the Government House event but was just as friendly.

Jodie Haydon told me she had been following what I was going through on social media, which blew me away. I was always surprised when someone with a busy life knew what was happening with my treatment. Katie and I chatted to 'Albo', as he's affectionately known in Sydney's inner west where we live, and we had our photos taken with him. The kids, who couldn't come to this event because of the restricted numbers, were proud when they saw he'd posted a photo of us on Instagram.

When we had lived in Newtown, Albo had lived a few doors away, though we didn't know him then. I once ran into him—he was then our local federal MP—when we were both waiting for takeaway from Surjit's Indian Restaurant in Annandale. For a few minutes we'd had a passionate discussion about some big political issue of the time, until our food arrived and we went our separate ways.

Then there were media interviews and more photos before a lunch at the National Gallery of Australia, where last year's Australian of the Year, body-image campaigner Taryn Brumfitt, made a speech. I sought out Keiren Perkins, the Olympic swimming legend who was chief executive of the Australian Sports Commission, to tell him about our campaign for sun safety in sport. He knew about it already and was keen to get involved.

We were supposed to have a few hours off in the afternoon but Georgina and I had to (finally!) practise our speech. We ran through it three times, making slight adjustments each time. Then, agreeing we weren't going to win anyway, we cut our practice short.

When we got dressed at the hotel, Katie and the kids looked sensational. After having some family photos taken, we hopped on the shuttle bus and arrived at the National Arboretum in the early evening to an almost overwhelming amount of fanfare. After another beautiful smoking ceremony, we walked down the red carpet with photographers stopping us for pics. I had a taste of what it must be like to be famous when we had our photos taken. While not exactly comfortable, we were quietly amused at how our lives had changed. The photographers asked for different combinations—Katie and me, the whole family, Georgina and me—before we headed inside.

I knew these would be great memories to hold onto forever. Maybe I didn't have a forever but, win or lose, this would be an experience the kids could tell their children about. For a moment, I remembered that my broken neck could have stopped me even coming to Canberra, and I felt very glad that I'd made it.

We were shown to tables near the stage. Katie, Emily and I sat together, with Matt and Lucy sitting with Western Australian nominee Mechelle Turvey and her sister Robyn Corbett. Having forged a sense of comradeship during the week with the other nominees and their families around us, we wished each other good luck.

The Village Centre, with its rock walls and spectacular vaulted wood-and-glass ceiling, was abuzz with formally dressed guests and waiters. TV cameras glided around, lining up shots. After a warm Welcome to Country by Aunty Violet Sheridan, the very deserving winners of the first three categories were announced. David Elliott, the co-founder of the Australian Age of Dinosaurs Museum in the Queensland town of Winton, was named Local Hero of the Year. He had really boosted the rural town with his vision, passion and hard work in setting up the museum.

Champion swimmer Emma McKeon won Young Australian of the Year. She is one of the country's best ever swimmers, a five-time world champion who had already won five Olympic gold medals. While my young doctor friend Nikhil missed out, Emma, having achieved so much in sport before turning 30, was a worthy winner.

I was a little nervous as our category drew closer but there was so much to enjoy about the awards. Aboriginal teacher, linguist and community leader Yalmay Yunupingu won Senior Australian of the Year. Her commitment to and passion for improving the lives of Aboriginal children without seeking the limelight was incredible. These were all outstanding people and, in the case of David and Yalmay, it struck me that their achievements would not be known outside their communities without the Australian of the Year awards.

Yalmay was joined on stage when accepting her award by someone whose company I'd enjoyed in Canberra: Witiyana Mariki, the Northern Territory's Local Hero. Along with

Yalmay's late husband, Witiyana had been a founding member of the rock band Yothu Yindi. We had chatted at some events and, just before the ceremony tonight, he had needed a hand tying his tie. I couldn't do it backwards so I stood behind him to knot it as he crouched. It was a nice human moment amid the formality.

Witiyana sent a charge through the room when, to rapt silence, he played clapsticks before Yalmay's moving speech. It struck me how difficult it must be for the judges to choose between all the nominees for Australian of the Year. Like Nikhil, Witiyana would have been a worthy winner in his category.

My heart was in my throat when it was time for our award. People had told Georgina and me that we were in with a chance but, while I thought we'd done important work, we didn't expect to win. I glanced at Katie and the kids.

The prime minister opened the envelope: 'The 2024 Australian of the Year, I'm proud to announce, is Professor Georgina Long and Professor Richard Scolyer.'

Fireworks went off inside my head. I stood, kissed Katie and the girls, hugged Matt and walked to the stage with Georgina amid handshakes and warm applause. We were both overwhelmed by a standing ovation.

Then came the speech we'd rehearsed without expecting we would need it. We acknowledged the Ngunnawal people, who were the traditional custodians of the land we had gathered on, and the other nominees who felt like friends now. 'We stand here tonight proudly representing every melanoma patient and their families, but also those with brain cancer and indeed all cancers,' I said. 'We share this incredible honour with a wonderful team and supporters at Melanoma Institute Australia, the world's leading melanoma research and clinical care facility.'

When we were planning our speech, Georgina and I had agreed with Institute communications head Jen Durante that it seemed like this would be the perfect platform to stress the importance of sun safety to a national audience on TV. 'Tomorrow, thousands of Aussies will be soaking up the sun, working on their tans,' Georgina said. 'Or, as we see it, brewing their melanomas. When it comes to tanning, we are swimming outside the flags. A tan is skin cells in trauma from overexposure to UV radiation from the sun.

'There is *nothing* healthy about a tan. *Nothing*. Our bronzed-Aussie culture is actually killing us. So we call on advertisers and social media influencers: stop glamorising tanning! Or using it to sell or advertise or entertain. And to our fellow Australians, when you see it, call it out. *Demand change.*'

Georgina is a brilliant speaker, articulate and passionate. If we were going to get to zero deaths from melanoma, we had to change the culture of tanning. I continued with a call to push cancer-treatment boundaries, backed by science, with more clinical trials.

Then I got personal. 'I stand here tonight as a terminal brain cancer patient,' I said, feeling the room get even quieter. 'I'm only 57. I don't want to die.'

The emotion was almost too much—it always felt raw talking so directly about dying—but I continued.

'I love my life, my family, my work. I've so much more to do and to give. I'm one of the many thousands of cancer patients who've travelled this path and thousands will follow. Devising this world-first experimental treatment for my type of brain cancer was bold. For me, the decision to take on Georgina's groundbreaking plan was a no-brainer. Here was an opportunity for us to crack another incurable cancer and make a difference—if not for me then for others.'

After Georgina explained that clinical trials were likely to follow—laboratory analysis of my tests would be used to make the case for subsequent clinical trials—I pressed on: 'From where I stand, with a future now measured in months rather than decades, it's impossible for me to properly articulate how proud and hopeful this makes me.'

Georgina urged Australians to do what we'd done—'think big, be bold, be courageous and . . . work together'—and, as a nation, to never let fear hold us back.

When I wrapped up by saying how much we appreciated the unwavering love from our families, and thanked Georgina for her passion, guidance and determination, she said something that still rattled me months later. 'Richard,' she said, 'I hope for nothing more than the both of us, in twelve months' time, to be standing here, passing the baton to the next Australian of the Year.'

I felt so many emotions—humility, joy, pride, love and momentary despair that I may not make it to a year—as we received another standing ovation. What an honour. What an unlikely reward for decades of work out of the public eye. What a moment for everyone we loved, as much as for us.

The other winners—David, Emma and Yalmay—joined us on stage as the ceremony finished with Jem Cassar-Daley singing a beautiful version of Crowded House's 'Something So Strong'.

The next half-hour was a blur: quick media interviews beside the stage, rejoining Katie and the kids, congratulations from all directions, being steered through a pumping dance floor to a live ABC Radio interview, then finding some quiet time in a small room where the head of the National Australia Day Council, Mark Fraser, and publicist Nicole Browne talked to us about how our lives were about to change. 'It's been a bit of a wild ride, right?' Mark said. I couldn't argue with that.

It was already way past my anti-epileptic-induced bedtime, but Nicole said we had to be in the hotel foyer at 5.10 a.m. for a full-on schedule of back-to-back interviews at Parliament House. As I tried to process everything that had happened and everything that would happen in— I checked my watch—*seven hours*, I saw that Emily, a keen swimmer, was thrilled to be meeting Emma McKeon at the other end of the room, and Katie, Matt and Lucy were enjoying taking it all in.

I was half asleep on Friday morning, and I don't drink coffee, but I came to life when the interviews started at

6.30 a.m. for Georgina and me. After 30 minutes with ABC local radio, we rolled on to ABC NewsRadio, ABC TV's *News Breakfast*, *Sunrise* on the Seven Network, Sky News, *Today* on the Nine Network, ABC Radio National's *RN Breakfast*, 2GB's Ben Fordham, then 6PR Perth. Every interview was different but the common subjects were in our bones—the dangers of skin cancer, the difference we were trying to make and my brain cancer treatment. The elation of the night before carried us through the early-morning schedule. We felt grateful, honoured, humbled, excited and, still, stunned by the award.

By 9 a.m., we were at a citizenship ceremony by Lake Burley Griffin. After the moving experience of seeing proud new Australians receiving their citizenship, we watched a helicopter trailing an Australian flag flying past and listened to a 21-gun salute. We were delighted to see the prime minister and many other VIPs wearing hats to protect their skin from the sun on another warm morning. I made a mental note to suggest they have more shade cover for guests next year.

Then Katie and I were spirited away to the Qantas Chairman's Lounge at Canberra airport—another new experience—on the way to Sydney for the Australia Day Live concert outside the Opera House. There were generous congratulations and friendly requests for selfies wherever we went.

There were also more interviews later in the day, for

10 News and *The Project* on the Ten Network. Presenter Kate Langbroek momentarily threw me when she cited an old saying I'd never heard before during our *Project* interview. 'They say a wise man plants a tree under which he will never sit,' she said. 'And we, and the rest of Australia, really hope that you get to sit under the tree that you have made for all of us.'

It was a touching thought, making me feel like everyone was on my side. I hoped I'd get to sit under that tree with my kids.

Before the concert, I loved seeing Emily, Matt and Lucy getting photos with the prime minister and NSW premier Chris Minns. We were taken to VIP seats—another first!—for a concert of classic Australian songs being performed by Mark Callaghan from GANGgajang, Dami Im, William Barton, Kate Miller-Heidke, Casey Donovan and other talents. I started to feel cold so I had to move inside, with Mark Fraser from the National Australia Day Council keeping me company. Feeling cold could mean a seizure was coming on but thankfully I was okay.

Having been up since 4.30 a.m., I could only just stay awake until we were called on stage for an interview with the ABC's Jeremy Fernandez for the telecast. When it was over, I realised I had to go home immediately.

The Council had lined up a golf buggy to take me through the crowd to meet a driver but I needed to go immediately, before the kids were ready to leave, so I said I'd walk.

A surprised policewoman organised a scrum of officers around me as I headed to Macquarie Street. I was too tired to appreciate the novelty of this experience, which had been crazily unimaginable—yet another first!—just a few days before.

Then home. And exhausted sleep.

———————

I woke early, as always. With the rest of the family asleep, I decided to head to the regular Saturday Parkrun—walking this time. While I didn't need the exercise, I did need to decompress after the busyness of the past few days. I also needed some normality and, deep down, I wanted to get to 200 Parkruns while I still could. I was at over 190 already but I didn't know how many more I'd be around for.

There was a fuss of some kind at the start but I couldn't make out what was being said in the fair-sized crowd, so I set off to walk-and-maybe-jog-just-a-little on the grass beside the path. I still had a broken neck so I didn't want to jar it. As I reached the finish—embarrassed by how slow I'd been—I saw other runners lining the finish chute. It was a guard of honour! I almost cried as they warmly applauded me over the line, struck once again by how kind and caring people were. I spent the next few minutes accepting congratulations and well wishes.

From one Parkrun to the next, something exceptional had happened. I wasn't famous like some of the people I'd been mixing with in Canberra, but I'd become better known. It felt like people I didn't know, who wouldn't have recognised me seven days ago, were on my side. It felt like they wanted me to get through this. I hoped I could.

11

BACK TO TREATMENT

I'm not sure what it was like for Weary Dunlop, Fred Hollows or Cathy Freeman after they won Australian of the Year, but I had a full book of medical appointments starting with my eleventh dose of immunotherapy—all three drugs after my liver-function tests had stabilised—the next Monday morning.

Hooked up to an IV drip at the Patricia Ritchie Centre for cancer care opposite the Institute, I was still on a high from the ceremony, the celebrations that followed and what the award meant in terms of taking our research and our 'zero deaths from melanoma' mission even further.

I was so appreciative of the recognition for Georgina and me, and so grateful for all the warmth behind the endless congratulations since our award had been announced. I was even more grateful for how much my parents, Katie and the kids had done for me over the years.

It struck me how profoundly we owed the pioneers of melanoma treatment in Australia, including Gerry Milton, Helen Shaw, Bill McCarthy, Vince McGovern and my mentors Stan McCarthy and John Thompson. The advances that Georgina and I had made with the exceptional team at the Institute had only been possible because of their ground-breaking work dating back to the 1960s.

The kids all came back to Sydney—Matt would soon be joining Emily in studying health sciences at the Australian National University in Canberra—and we enjoyed watching highlights of the ABC's Australian of the Year broadcast and seeing photos on social media from the week's celebrations.

I couldn't keep up with the hundreds of text messages from colleagues, friends, acquaintances and supporters who had been following how we'd been trying to revolutionise brain cancer treatment. I responded to as many as I could. But what nobody outside my family and medical team knew was that I was going through the toughest three weeks since I'd started treatment, with a new anti-epileptic drug leaving me feeling very tired and lethargic.

I'd sparked up when I had to in Canberra—drinking a Coke sometimes helped—but felt awful at other times. I'd been falling asleep during the day and struggling to function, with the exhaustion coming on top of a runny nose and blocked ears that seemed to be getting worse.

Helen Wheeler had prescribed the new drug after another setback that came out of the blue: I had a third short seizure, losing consciousness and passing out in the lounge room when I was at home with Matt and Lucian, the partner of Katie's sister Sally. I had the usual symptoms I'd get before a partial seizure but this time I blacked out. I was sitting on the couch at the time and woke up with Matt going, 'Dad, Dad!'

So, rather than wildly celebrating our win, I was wondering what was going to happen in the coming year. The odds were that it was going to be a tough time.

Then, before I knew it, there was another moment of truth—my next brain scan.

How I approached scans had changed as the months passed. I had often been asked whether I had 'scanxiety'— anxiety about a coming scan—given their significance in detecting tumour recurrence. My approach had been to keep busy with family, work and exercise, so that I didn't think too much about a possibly dire outcome. Even with the draining effects of the new anti-epileptic drug, I still tried to keep busy. But if I'd been sitting at home all day every day, I would definitely have been more anxious.

This time, it was the familiar routine of being scanned then waiting a day or two for the results. Happily, I was clear again! There was no sign of tumour recurrence after eight months—two months more than the median time. It was still way too early to know if immunotherapy was stopping the tumour coming back—radiotherapy could have delayed it, or I might just have been lucky so far—but the scan result was a huge boost.

For a while I'd felt the scans would show the tumour returning before there was any other sign, like a full-on seizure caused by it growing in my brain. But Helen was concerned that I was still having partial seizures even with the high dose of anti-epileptic medication I was on. Could these episodes be caused by the immunotherapy, the radiotherapy or possibly the tumour returning? We didn't know.

Everyone at the Institute was upbeat at a celebratory morning tea for the Australian of the Year award after the multidisciplinary team meeting the next Friday morning. Given how much they had contributed to what we had achieved, it was fantastic to share our success with them.

When colleagues asked me how I was feeling, I answered with honesty and openness—always my attitude—but being a glioblastoma rather than a melanoma patient, my care was never discussed at these meetings.

While I hadn't been able to return to all my pathology duties at RPA, I was delighted that—in addition to my work at the Institute, my research and my medical appointments—I could still contribute opinions on difficult cases for an anatomical pathology team that I'd enjoyed working with over the years. They include a group who had genuine expertise in melanoma pathology—Dr Robert Rawson, Dr Peter Ferguson, Dr Andrew Colebatch and Dr Alison Potter—and it was a pleasure to keep up our connection.

Away from the spotlight, Katie, who was still on leave from work, made sure the kids felt supported and could talk about the emotions they were going through. Having dinner with them, we would give them updates on my treatment and make sure they felt like they were able to ask whatever questions they had. Time we spent together as a family eating, watching TV, playing sport or even just going for a walk felt more valuable than ever before. They were the most important people in my life, and I didn't know how long I'd get to spend with them.

———————

As winners of Australian of the Year, Georgina and I received requests to get involved in various events but they weren't demanding or even compulsory, and they gave us a new platform to promote our work. When it came to the many media requests, we were happy to spread the news about our melanoma progress and our radical brain cancer treatment internationally when there was an opportunity. In an interview with *Sky News Breakfast* in the UK, Georgina said we had shown neoadjuvant immunotherapy could activate the immune system for glioblastoma and 'this is now a foundational first step to change the field and the way drugs are explored in brain cancer'.

Asked how I was feeling, I was positive: 'The risks of major adverse reactions to these sorts of drugs is fairly high but I've had plain sailing so far, so I couldn't be happier and hope it stays like that for some time longer.'

We were keen to share our clinical findings on immune cell activation after pre-surgery combination immunotherapy on my tumour in an international journal. The publicly available report, which was going through peer review, said in scientific terms that 'we show for the first time that neoadjuvant inhibition of triple immune checkpoints in newly diagnosed GBM (glioblastoma) markedly increased the diversity, abundance and activation of TILs (tumor-infiltrating lymphocytes, which are immune cells that can recognise and kill cancer cells), compared with the baseline tumor before treatment.' We added that there was an 'urgent need to investigate this strategy in clinical trials'. Georgina had already started planning—in September 2023—the first clinical trial to see how well immunotherapy before surgery worked for a large group of glioblastoma patients.

Georgina and I seemed to be making regular visits to Canberra, and not just for Australian of the Year events.

In February, we had meetings with Prime Minister Anthony Albanese in Sydney then in Canberra, with federal education minister Jason Clare, health and aged care minister Mark Butler and independent MP and paediatric neurologist Monique Ryan.

We wanted to encourage the federal government to act on a range of important measures: modernising the sun-safety message, stopping the glamorisation of tanning, promoting more sun safety in sport, emphasising the importance of checking your own skin—'know the skin you're in'—and developing a screening program for people at high risk of getting melanoma.

We also met US ambassador to Australia Caroline Kennedy. She presented Georgina, who had taken up a Fulbright Postdoctoral Fellowship at the Scripps Research Institute in the

US earlier in her career, with the US Mission Australia Award for Leadership Excellence.

It felt like a productive visit. We hoped to see measures to help us reach zero deaths from melanoma introduced in the coming months.

After my heartfelt interviews with *A Current Affair* then *Australian Story*, I found myself revealing the rawness of my emotions on a podcast with broadcaster Neil Mitchell. Mentioning Georgina's comment that Brindha 'hadn't taken the Richard out of Richard' in the debulking surgery, he asked whether the operation had had any effect on me.

'It affected me emotionally I think more than anything,' I said. 'But as far as my brain function goes, it doesn't seem to have. I've been having a whole heap of neuro-cognitive testing. I had one the day before I went into surgery. And I do better on most tests now than I did in the one before surgery. I'm not saying I've got more brain power—and it's not the same test—but I was stressed before I had the major surgery.'

My being more emotional could be simply down to having an incurable cancer. But the side effects of medication, the location of the tumour in the amygdala, which can affect your emotions, and having less independence might also be factors, I explained.

Did I cry more easily?

'Definitely I cry more easily than normal,' I said, thinking of the times I'd been overtaken by sadness, fear, anxiety and frustration since I was first diagnosed. 'Sometimes I'm more agitated than I normally would be. The people closest to you are the ones who have to ride that. Realistically, it's Katie who would cop it more than anyone. It's not a big issue but it's more than normal.'

I tried to explain what had changed. 'Things that I normally like to do, I can't do. That disappoints me. And even how I prioritise what I want to get through in a day—it's different to what I'd do in the past. I guess I was very focused on work and very proud of what we were doing. I still [am], to some degree, but I just don't have the time to churn out things like I have in the past.'

Since Poland, I'd cried with Katie and the kids. I'd cried when we'd all watched TV interviews that brought home how lethal my brain cancer was. I'd cried at the thought that I'd leave my kids without a dad and that I'd miss important times in their lives—graduations, birthdays, falling in love, maybe having children of their own. I'd cried thinking about how I'd upturned Katie's life. I've cried working on this book and reflecting on my mum's struggles and my dad's devotion to her.

Neil mentioned talking to a terminally ill person who had said their illness was like a gift for a while. It gave more clarity to their life. They knew what mattered and, even though their illness was going to kill them, they felt it had been beneficial in that way. Had my brain tumour given me any of that perspective or clarity?

'I hear what you're saying, and I can appreciate that, but if I'm brutally honest, I don't feel I've got there yet. I think I should be there,' I said. 'This is where I need to go. But I'm not there yet.'

In truth, I don't know when or even if I'll reach the stage of accepting that my brain cancer is terminal. As soon as Georgina gave me a slim chance by trying immunotherapy, I wanted to fight it. As a doctor, I want to keep moving forward, seeing what's possible in terms of finding a cure for this devastating cancer. As a scientist, I want to keep trying treatments and generating data that could help other patients. As a husband and father, I want to be around for my family for as long as possible.

I know the tumour is likely to come back—chances are it will be within months—but I'm a long way from thinking it's been a gift. I loved my life before I was diagnosed—my family, my work, the fact we'd made major progress in saving lives from melanoma, my friends, my colleagues, exercising. I absolutely hate what glioblastoma has done to it.

Neil asked whether my mother's illness had affected my life.

'A hundred per cent, it affected my life,' I said. 'I went and lived with an aunty and uncle who were on a farm in the countryside in Tasmania. To be living without your parents for some months—trying to make do—definitely made me learn ways to cope. I guess in some ways, coping in isolation.

'When there were problems, you just had to deal with them. I'm sure that's had an impact on me and my life. I hadn't actually considered any of this stuff until the cancer journey started. In some respects, it's probably been a reason why I've been successful in what I've done. I don't get hung up on some things that perhaps other people would . . . when there

---

are emotional issues that people get peeved with someone else about. I tend to be able to move on pretty quickly and focus on the big goals.'

For a pathologist who had spent decades talking in public about data and public health campaigns, I was now having to reflect emotionally on life and death, not just privately but in public. I found this difficult, so I appreciated how well people responded when I spoke openly about my feelings.

Physically (if not emotionally), I started to feel strong again as the weeks went on. My broken neck had healed, although my neck flexibility was not as good as it had been before, and my general health had improved. I'd been preparing to ride the first three days of the Tour de Cure, a cancer-fundraising event in Tassie in March, but my training had been disrupted. So I got back on the bike and went for a ride early one morning at Sydney Olympic Park with the Balance triathlon club. Exercising always made me feel better, in every way.

March was also a big month for the Institute.

We had what we called Melanoma March events around the country that drew attention to the importance of sun safety, supported patients, remembered those who had died from skin cancer and raised funds for research. In an interview about these events on the Seven Network's *Morning Show*, I hammered home the idea that tanning was skin cells in trauma.

'We've got to change our behaviour to reduce the risk of people developing melanoma,' I said. 'Ninety per cent of [melanomas] are caused by ultraviolet damage to the skin. We don't want people to stop enjoying Australia—we live in this incredible country—it's just to be smart about what you do. Don't go out in the middle of the day where you can help it, do things when the sun is not at its strongest and wear protective clothing. Put on hats, sunglasses, sunscreen where [skin is] exposed.'

To mark our Australian of the Year win, Georgina and I were scheduled to host a Melanoma March event at the Bay Run I knew so well, in the inner west of Sydney: a 4-kilometre walk and 7-kilometre jog. It was the first time a Melanoma March event was held there and we had hundreds of people of all ages signing up.

When I had a check-up with Georgina, she said it sounded like I was coughing up phlegm and asked what colour it was. I told her it was green. She examined my lungs and suggested a CAT scan of my chest, which showed a new health issue: I had bilateral lower lobe pneumonia.

I had hoped to get in some good training for the Tour de Cure by this time, but the illness I'd caught just after Christmas hadn't cleared up. It had also affected my sinuses—causing gross mucosal swelling—and subsequently I'd developed a phlegmy cough that made Georgina suspect that the infection had spread to my lungs.

I still had a blocked nose and could feel viscid (thick and sticky) fluid in my ears, which made me anxious that I was going to get a middle ear infection, as well as some minor skin rashes, and I was still anaemic. These symptoms were likely side effects of immunotherapy. I started a course of antibiotics for the pneumonia then used a steroid inhaler to reduce my sinonasal mucosal swelling.

While I'd continued losing weight from feeling sick and not eating as much—I was down to 73 kilograms—my energy levels had gradually improved and, with the new anti-epileptic medication, I was less tired and stopped having to sleep so much.

I didn't feel short of breath and could still exercise pretty much as usual, so I went for a long Saturday bike ride with the Sydney Tour de Cure training group, covering 127 kilometres from home to West Head in the Ku-ring-gai Chase National Park, then back via the northern beaches. I wasn't having a perfect preparation for the Tassie ride but at least I was getting some kilometres into my legs.

Before leaving for Tassie, Georgina and I—wearing the smart new wide-brimmed hats that Akubra had given us after our Australian of the Year win—launched our new Melanoma March Bay Run event on a warm Sunday morning, giving a speech about why these activities were vital fundraisers that paid tribute to melanoma patients and their families.

I had planned an easy 7-kilometre jog around the Bay Run loop but my good friend Trevor Murphy, who had become visually impaired in recent years with a genetic disorder of the eyes called retinitis pigmentosa, was finding it tough getting through the crowd on the route, so I ran with him.

Trevor is a talented athlete who I'd trained with, on and off, for years. Leading into the Tokyo Paralympics, when he had hoped to qualify to represent Australia as a triathlete, another friend, Fraser Turvey, and I swam, cycled and ran with him as guides in qualifying events. Unfortunately, Trevor just missed out on qualifying, possibly because his guides lacked the horsepower that he had.

On that Melanoma March day, Trevor and I ended up running at a quicker-than-planned pace of just over five minutes per kilometre. Normally that would be easily manageable but I'd only found out I had pneumonia two days earlier. When we returned to the start of the run at Rodd Point, there were people to meet and photos to be taken, so I didn't get a chance to drink or eat until I was parched and hungry. Back home, after breakfast and a few hours of recovery, I packed up my bike and headed to the airport for the Tassie ride.

In Launceston, before the Tour de Cure started, I caught up with my parents. Because Dad had just had COVID and I had pneumonia, I couldn't risk staying with him, so we spent time together outside, rather than inside his house, talking. My friend Jim Finlay and his wife Liz O'Donahue put me up at their place, which was near Mum's nursing home, and, not being able to drive because of my seizures, I rode my bike everywhere.

Jim and the legendary Richie Porte were also riding the Tour de Cure. It turned out to be a tremendous event. Many of the riders had lost loved ones to cancer and wanted to raise funds for research. As we rolled out in Hobart, in different groups, I did my best to stay upright on the bike while being interviewed on TV. Jim waited with me until my interview commitments were over. With the peloton kilometres down the road, we needed a lift in a van to catch up.

It was always fantastic riding in Tassie, with the fresh air and the beautiful scenery. There was extraordinarily friendly company on the ride and enthusiastic encouragement in the places we rode through and stopped at overnight. Day one was a long and steady ride of 110 kilometres from Hobart to Swansea; I managed that okay. Day two was 152 kilometres to Launceston, which I was pleased to make, and day three was a scenic 104 kilometres to Devonport.

It was a different experience to when I'd ridden with the Tour the previous year. I'd gone with the fastest group then and, with my competitive personality, I had chased the gun cyclists as they raced uphill—I couldn't help myself. That meant my legs had been smashed backing up the next day. This year, the ride was more controlled—slow and steady, with everyone sticking together—so I didn't find it as hard. The year before, I'd connected with other riders as a cancer researcher. This time, as a cancer patient as well as a researcher, the connections were even stronger.

I enjoyed everything about the Tour, including the fact it was a fundraiser for cancer research. As we passed through Riverside, I pointed out to riders near me the car park that I'd built, the schools I'd gone to and where my dad lived. I was far from the most famous Rich from Riverside there—that was Richie Porte—but I had as much fun as anyone.

While it wasn't a competitive event—quite the opposite—I still found myself wanting to push it at times. Since my diagnosis, which had forced me to be more reflective about my life, I had sometimes wondered where this competitiveness, this drive to succeed, came from.

Was it genetic or the result of my upbringing? Maybe it came from the difficulties I had as a kid when Mum was away and I learned I had to do things myself while staying with Lily and Roy on that remote farm for so long. I'm not good at psychology but I think that experience could have had a different impact on me—another kid might have felt abandoned. But Mark and I had so much love from our parents that, when we were all back together again in Launceston, I was able to get on with life and chase my goals. Maybe my ambition came from striving for attention from my parents, or maybe it was just my personality to want to be the best I could be.

While I've tried to downplay it, I know that deep inside I've been very driven for as long as I can remember. It has helped me be successful, striving to be good at my job and have an impact on the world stage—carrying out further research, taking on increasing work responsibilities and honorary roles, pushing to improve diagnosis and refine the accuracy of prognoses so that patients have the best chance of getting the medical treatment they need and deserve.

I feel fortunate that I don't seem to get upset by the dramas or conflicts that irritate other people. Or, if I do, they don't take up too much of my mental energy.

What I've learned, though, is that if you want to get good at something, you keep practising it. You stay committed to making things happen. You focus on the major goal and don't worry about little things. Whether you're successful is partly down to luck and opportunity. But it also comes down to the characteristics you've inherited—intelligence is important, but what matters most is what you do with your talent, how you get on with people and whether you can get them on board to work together as a team.

Teamwork is important, as is living up to all those values that I admired in my mentors Stan McCarthy and John Thompson: dedication, humility, hard work, encouraging other people, mentoring the next generation, valuing the expertise of others, caring for your patients.

Are there downsides to my competitiveness? Undoubtedly.

I've long wanted to excel at whatever I am doing, whether in the lab, at the Institute or writing up a research paper. Even with endurance sports like triathlon and cycling, I've always enjoyed participating, but they have sucked up too much time because I've always wanted to push myself to get better at them.

The cancer diagnosis gave me the perspective to see that I often worked too hard and didn't take as much time off for family and leisure as I should have. But I couldn't just take a holiday when I came to that realisation. The kids were all studying and there were any number of medical appointments every week. I found the best approach was to continue doing the things I love, while enjoying as much time with my family as I could.

I wanted to keep contributing as a pathologist and co-medical director of the Institute, pushing towards zero deaths from melanoma and trying to revolutionise glioblastoma treatment. And, when I could, I wanted to continue with research, exercise and activities, including speaking commitments and media interviews, that drew attention to our work. It always feels like there are new ways to contribute to medicine and get better outcomes for patients.

I've tried to show my love more openly to my family since my diagnosis—to hug them, text them, call them, help the kids with their schoolwork, spend more time with them. I must have been a pain for the people around me sometimes, but I just hope I've been able to show everyone how much I love them.

———

After arriving back from Tassie on a Sunday night, I had my next brain scan first up the next morning. After all that cycling—not just the physical exertion but the many inspiring conversations I'd had along the way—I had no problem with scanxiety.

My diagnosis and treatment had been the subject of the final episode of *Australian Story* in 2023. With so much happening since then, including the Australian of the Year award, the crew were back filming an updated episode. They met me at home and shot footage as I went for my scan at St Leonards. It added a little more complexity to life over the coming days when they filmed Georgina and me at the Institute, but they'd made a good show first time around so I went with their requests.

The scan results were again fantastic—now ten months without recurrence! I was thrilled. Was immunotherapy having a clinical benefit? It was still too early to say but maybe there was a sliver more hope. I shared the news on social media and saw from the hundreds of comments how many people were delighted not just for me but for what it could mean for future brain cancer patients.

To stay honest and open, I posted again a few days later to say that it hadn't all been plain sailing lately.

I mentioned that I'd had inflammation and swelling in my nose and sinuses for a couple of months, an upper respiratory infection, a lower respiratory infection that had turned out to be bilateral pneumonia, and dips in my blood test results for liver function and cardiac enzymes, which meant Georgina had delayed my next immunotherapy dose. My doses had been delayed before—it was her call as the medical oncologist looking after my immunotherapy—but hopefully my blood tests would get back to normal and I'd get the next dose soon.

In the April school holidays, Katie and I took Lucy for a break by the beach at Coolum on Queensland's Sunshine Coast. We thoroughly enjoyed it and I felt the best physically that I had for months. On the way back to Sydney, I spoke at a Tour de Cure lunch in Brisbane to say thanks for all the funds they'd raised for cancer research. I said that immunotherapy breakthroughs had meant that 57 per cent of advanced melanoma patients were now alive for five years, with most effectively cured (which means we believe it won't return), and our focus was on helping the remaining patients. I cited a major hope that we had been working on.

'We believe that personalised immunotherapy is the key—identifying the right treatment for the right patient, at the right time,' I said. At the Institute, the research team had developed what we called the Personalised Immunotherapy Platform (PIP), which used a patient's individual biomarkers to predict how tumours would respond to standard immuno-therapy, and allowed us to quickly identify patients who were not likely to respond and could possibly be given novel therapies earlier.

This platform had the potential to not only transform treatment for advanced melanoma patients but to revolu-tionise the treatment of other cancers across the globe. 'As a pathologist and researcher,' I said, 'this is what excites me about the path ahead.'

I also spoke about my own experience as a cancer researcher and clinician with a terminal diagnosis: 'Maybe I'm too much of an optimist but my deep scientific under-standing allowed me to view my own diagnosis through a different lens.' I noted that I didn't know what the future held for me. 'I love my life, and have so much still to do, and to give,' I said. 'Let me leave you with this: no matter what life throws at you, seek out opportunities to contribute, to participate and to action change. As I like to say, "have a crack". And don't just lean in. Leap in.'

As always, I felt emotional and raw talking in public about life and death. It was a crowd of people who already knew the value of cancer research and believed in the work we were doing, and I appreciated their standing ovation.

––––––

During my treatment, I hadn't had the luxury of looking too far ahead. The focus had always been on what was happening immediately and in the short-term future. I never knew how many months I had left to live.

But after getting to ten months without recurrence and having had the eighth of ten doses of my personal cancer vaccine, there was an offer a little further into the future that I wanted to accept. It was more hope than optimism, but why not?

Triathlon Australia had a team competing in the world age-group multisport championships in Townsville in August. After our Australian of the Year win, they had invited me to join the team and, with Georgina, carry the flag at the opening ceremony, which was a beautiful gesture. I wanted to represent Australia again, even it was just for one last time. It would also mean a lot if the kids could join me, turning it into a family experience that they would remember.

I accepted the invitation, and Triathlon Australia found spots for Emily and Matt in races where Australian triathletes hadn't filled all the available places. I ordered the new-style Australian triathlon suit, which, after our lobbying, would cover my back, shoulders and upper arms. Just two more clear brain scans and I could hopefully race!

Katie and I also decided we'd head to Winton in outback Queensland for an Australian of the Year event in May with the Local Hero David Elliott, the co-founder of the Australian Age of Dinosaurs museum, who had been a real character when we met him in Canberra. While I'd been invited to speak at the American Society of Clinical Oncology annual meeting in Chicago, heading to somewhere we'd never visited in Australia was more appealing.

Just before my twelve-month scans, a package arrived in the mail. It was a copy of a new textbook that I had written with Klaus Busam, my dermatopathologist friend from New York, called *Melanocytic Tumors of the Skin*. I had always felt proud seeing my name on the cover of a new book for the first time. This time, I felt proud seeing my name on the cover of a new book for probably the last time. I didn't want to measure life in 'last' experiences but sometimes these markers were impossible to avoid.

12

THE HOPEFUL FUTURE

A biopsy by open craniotomy, thirteen cycles of immuno-therapy (including five with three drugs), 30 sessions of radiotherapy, eight anti-cancer vaccine injections, a six-hour tumour debulking operation, five lumbar punctures and hundreds of blood tests.

After an intense series of treatments—up to May 2024—my MRI scan at twelve months showed no recurrence of the tumour. While delighted to get through my previous scans, this time there was a real turnaround in my emotions. I couldn't believe how overjoyed I felt.

I went out to dinner to celebrate with Katie, close family and friends at a Greek restaurant at Potts Point. It was a year to the day since I'd had my first seizure in Poland, and

I was so happy to share a meal with people I love. I made a speech to say how much I had appreciated all the support from everyone, including my brother Mark and his partner Anna, who had moved from Melbourne to Sydney in recent weeks to be closer to us.

I was relieved a few hours before that dinner to take off an electroencephalogram (EEG) that I'd been wearing for five days. It was a sci-fi-looking device that attached twenty electrodes to my scalp under a bandana, with the wires connecting to a pouch that went around my neck. My neurologist, Dr Kaitlyn Parratt, wanted to check for so-called subclinical seizures—partial seizures you can have without realising—and monitor other brain activity. I couldn't shower or exercise and it was difficult to sleep while wearing the EEG, so I wasn't sad to see it go.

For virtually all of the last year, I had regarded my diagnosis as a straight path to death. Probably every day I thought about how little time I had left and what this would mean for my family. I hated how the tumour had overturned my life. I was angry and sad that I might have months instead of decades with family and friends, that I couldn't work and exercise like I'd always done, that I couldn't even drive anymore. I feared that my brain tumour would recur, and I'd be counting the good days I had left before I started to decline.

I never expected to reach twelve months with no sign of the tumour coming back. And now that I'm here, I can't believe I'm still around and basically functioning like I used to.

But I'm not out of the woods, by a long way. While the median time to recurrence for my aggressive type of glioblastoma is six months, some patients who go through the standard treatment do get to twelve months without recurrence. It's too early to say if my world-first treatment—combination immunotherapy before surgical debulking and a personalised cancer vaccine—has worked to stop the tumour returning. There needs to be scientific evidence over a longer term, which means clinical trial data, and there isn't any at this stage.

At the start of treatment, I thought there might be a 5 per cent chance at best that immunotherapy would be effective and extend my life. I thought the chances of me being cured were less than 1 per cent. I have no idea whether my chances have improved but I feel as good as gold.

Even so, I'm naturally still apprehensive about the future. I expect that's true for all cancer patients going through treatment.

Whatever the reason I'm here, I'm delighted to have had a whole year of life with my family. I'm now very confident of reaching fourteen months (the median *survival* for my type of glioblastoma) without recurrence. Even late last year, I didn't think that was remotely possible.

I feel lucky. Blessed. Definitely more optimistic. I hope I'm not deluded but I reckon I'm going to continue the life I've been leading for the rest of 2024. From the time of writing, that would be seven more priceless months.

One of the reasons I feel so upbeat is that I've now come through a tough eight or so weeks, from mid-January to

March, when the increased dosage of anti-epileptic drugs, then the transition from one drug to another, really knocked me around. I felt so exhausted and sluggish that I wondered if having the partial seizures, which the drugs were meant to stop, would have been better.

For four weeks, my blood tests were also abnormal, so Georgina was hesitant about giving me any more immunotherapy. I didn't want the enzymes that leak out of my muscles during exercise being interpreted as coming from my liver, so I stopped running and riding. That wasn't ideal, given all the physical and emotional benefits I get from exercise, but immunotherapy was more important than fitness.

After my test results settled down and I had my thirteenth immunotherapy dose, I started exercising again and—another reason for feeling so encouraged—I've been surprised by how well I've gone.

It might not mean much to non-runners but, in early May, I ran the 5-kilometre Parkrun in 20 minutes, 39 seconds. That was my best time since last Christmas Day. Ever competitive, for better or worse, I want to break twenty minutes again soon.

I've also done some runs of around 15 kilometres at a decent pace, have been riding indoors on my home trainer and went for a 115-kilometre cycle to West Head and back. Having stayed out of the pool since I was diagnosed—because of the risk of having a seizure and possibly drowning—I even joined Lucy, our youngest daughter, for a short swim.

As well as just enjoying exercising again, I want to get in shape for the world multisport championships in Townsville in August. It's more than three months away as I write this but I'm still planning to race there with Emily and Matt.

When I accepted Triathlon Australia's offer to race, it was more out of hope than confidence that I'd be able to compete. Privately, I'd calculated that there was a good chance I'd still be alive and able to cheer for the kids, even if I wasn't well enough to participate. Now it feels like I'll be able to race and, if I can keep training, I shouldn't be too far off my normal level of fitness.

Amazing. It makes me feel so happy.

─────────

One big question we're asking now is how many more doses of immunotherapy I'll have. The short answer is: I'm not sure. There's been debate in my medical team about whether I need more doses, at the risk of further side effects. Evidence from melanoma patients, and from the pathology results from my debulking operation, suggests that my immune system is already somewhat activated to attack the tumour cells. So there might not be any further benefits of immunotherapy, and, on this argument, we should hold off further doses until the tumour recurs.

Happily I've been knocked around less than expected with *three* immunotherapy drugs, when the chance of a major side effect is 60 per cent with *two* drugs in melanoma patients.

In early June, data will be presented at the American Society of Clinical Oncology's annual meeting in Chicago on a clinical trial of 46 patients with advanced melanoma from different countries who have been treated with three immunotherapy drugs. The trial, on patients undergoing a median of five months of treatment, found 'encouraging efficacy' from the three drugs, although additional studies will be needed to confirm the results because of the small sample size. It will take more data to determine whether three drugs is more effective than two drugs and how they compare for side effects.

Since my first immunotherapy treatment, when I experienced intermittent high temperatures, vomiting and a rash, I've been extremely fortunate to have had mostly relatively minor side effects: dry skin and dry hair; a cold with a runny nose; blocked ears that were caused by sinusitis; and pneumonia, which was a complication of the sinusitis. However I did go on to have grade 3 liver toxicity, detected by significantly abnormal liver function tests, which is regarded as a serious adverse event.

I now think it's unlikely that the partial seizures I've had since arriving back from Poland were complications of immunotherapy. While not proven, my view is they were more likely to have been caused by radiotherapy, but they could also be caused by other treatments, including surgery and drug therapies, or even the location of the tumour in the temporal lobe.

The other complication during my treatment has been anaemia—a low haemoglobin level. Once we worked out that my iron deficiency was caused by me giving too much blood for testing and research, we reduced the volume of blood that was taken. When I started on iron tablets and had an iron infusion, it ceased being a problem.

Why have I had so few side effects? The major factor has to be good clinical care—Georgina knew what side effects to look out for and how to manage them. Other factors could include how well I am normally and the genes I inherited from my parents. Some people have suggested that being physically fit has helped, but there doesn't seem to be any data from clinical trials to back that. Some very fit young patients experience toxicity; some very inactive people have none.

While it took a long time to happen, I've started to think more about the future. Having unexpectedly had a whole year with Katie and the kids, I desperately want more time with them now. I'm a little regretful that I didn't spend enough time with them in the past. One small positive from a brain-tumour diagnosis is that it allows more months with your loved ones than, say, sudden death in an accident.

Katie has been saying for a while that she believes I'll still be around for Father's Day in September 2024. I was convinced I'd probably had my final Christmas last year but, incredibly, I'm now pretty confident I'll be around for another one this year.

Looking at it from a scientist's perspective, though, it is still likely that the tumour will come back. If and when it does, I would have eight months left, on average. No doubt, these eight months would be a difficult period of declining health, with the last two or three months dismal for both me and my family. So it's clear I have to make the most of whatever time I have left.

There are medical options if the tumour comes back. Brindha could operate again to take out some of the new bulk. But it wouldn't be as straightforward as it was the first time around. Because of the area she would need to operate on, damage to my brain function would be likely—it could mean the loss of my short-term memory, among other things.

When Georgina made that emotional declaration after the Australian of the Year announcement—'I hope for nothing more than the both of us, in twelve months' time, to be standing here, passing the baton to the next Australian of the Year'—it seemed an impossibility from my perspective. Another year? No chance.

But I now think I will be around then. I might be crook and even need a wheelchair to get on stage, but I believe it's realistic that I'll still be alive in eight months.

That's a stark contrast to how I felt when I was first diagnosed.

I was distressed that I wouldn't see our kids grow up. I remembered my relationship with my own parents—how exciting it was when I first went to uni and had all this freedom, meeting new people and experiencing a different life that was busy and fun. My parents' home—a two-hour drive away—often felt too far to go for a weekend when I had so many other social and sporting commitments. It was only in my later years at uni that I circled back, and my parents became a really important part of my life again. So, when I was first diagnosed, I thought about missing out on that time with my own kids as they grew into adults and made their own way in the world.

It's tremendous that Emily and Matt are at uni in Canberra—I'd never want my illness to stop them following their interests and enjoying that experience—but, unlike me in my early uni years, they have been coming back home regularly to spend time with the rest of the family. That shows what fantastic and caring young adults they have become. Lucy is halfway through Year 11, so she'll be finished high school in eighteen months. At home, it's also helped everyone's spirits that we now have our first family pet—an affectionate and excitable cavoodle pup named Cha-Cha. He's been a delight to have around.

How amazing will it be if I am able to be part of the kids' lives as they become adults? But that's just too far ahead in the future to imagine yet. For now, I cherish every extra week I have with them.

———

Whatever happens, I feel like there will be a legacy from what Georgina, our team and I have tried to do.

I'm proudest of the courage we've all shown to see if we can make a difference in brain cancer treatment. The risk I faced was that I'd die earlier than I would have under standard treatment. Georgina's risk was reputational damage if a friend and colleague died quickly under her care after she had tried an experimental treatment.

Our research findings suggest immunotherapy before surgery is worth further investigation, at the very least, for brain cancer patients. Georgina is working with neuro-oncologists to set up a clinical trial, partnering with cancer research organisations in Melbourne and the US, with the backing of a pharmaceutical company.

Feedback from the neuro-oncology community indicates we've given them hope for a new brain cancer treatment, even if there are risks associated with it.

But we need to integrate discoveries we have made in melanoma and other cancers into brain cancer research and treatment. That's how we can get the best possible outcome for patients.

Consider what might have happened in my case. If Polish doctors had decided I needed an urgent operation or had given me steroids for brain swelling, it would have had implications for my subsequent treatment back in Australia. I might not have been able to try neoadjuvant immuno-therapy or, if I had, it may have had a lower chance of being effective. If a neurosurgeon had done a core biopsy instead of a riskier open craniotomy, there may not have been enough tumour tissue for the type of cutting-edge research that our team has been doing. So much more was possible because we had a team of people working closely together.

While we don't know for certain, the longer I live, the more likely it seems that immunotherapy is doing what we've been hoping it will do. Georgina said earlier this year that she'd need me to survive for two years to feel like it has had the desired effect. But even if I'm around then, nothing will have been proven. Every now and then in melanoma, a patient is cured for no apparent reason. I could be in that fluky category for brain cancer. The only way to prove immunotherapy works is with a clinical trial.

Would I have done anything differently with my treatment, now that I've come this far? No. I'm comfortable that I received the right treatment.

What I've learned, though, is how much emotion comes with a cancer diagnosis. It's not something I've been exposed to before. Facing a lot of emotional issues has turned out to be the hardest part of having cancer—everyone around you suffers, especially your family. I'm disappointed in myself in one respect: I was so caught up in facing what seemed like certain death within fourteen months that I wasn't there for Katie as much as I should have been.

There has been a lot to deal with. Until I was diagnosed, I'd never really thought about who I am deep inside. Maybe I was too obsessed with work and what I could achieve— always looking forward, always trying to get things done, never looking back. That's changed.

I've always known that I was driven. That I was ambitious to do things, make things happen. That I worked too hard.

What I now know with more certainty is that my family, extended family and close friends are the most important things in my life. We've had many rich experiences together, but I feel like I've neglected my family sometimes and missed opportunities to spend time with them while I've been working or travelling for work. I'd encourage other driven people to think about what really matters, and spend more time with their families before it's too late.

Having reflected on my life in sessions with cancer psychologists, I've realised how much experiences from my childhood, especially my mother's ill health and being away from my family for more than six months while she received treatment, have had an effect on how I've acted as an adult. I think these early jolts made me more self-reliant and driven to achieve, possibly due to wanting recognition. And they also contributed to me sometimes running away from problems—hiding my emotions—rather than facing up to them directly.

Even with all the support I've had, it's still been really tough getting through easily the most challenging year of my life. I've been far from perfect. As well as being more tired than usual, I've found I've been less tolerant, more irritable and more emotional. Is this from the stress, the location of the tumour in my brain or the side effects of one of my treatments? Nobody really knows. I'm just grateful that, whatever the reason, I've been able to recognise it and still contribute at a high level in work, family life, social activities and sport.

———

The last year has also given me a lot more empathy for other cancer patients. Earlier in my medical career, I often treated patients with cancer and other life-threatening diseases. I did my best to help them. Then, when my shift finished, I got on with the rest of my life. But having an incurable cancer has been a totally different experience. I've learned that unless they have gone through the same situation, even the people closest to you don't know what facing a death sentence feels like. How could they? Even very caring people don't appreciate how it drills down deep into your core and affects you almost every minute of every day.

This empathy has made me more motivated to advocate for how governments, clinical teams and research organisations should spend their time and resources to do the most good for cancer patients.

Have I turned to religion or spirituality since my terminal diagnosis? I understand why some people do. For my own part, however, I wasn't brought up in a religious family and I'm a scientist. I recognise that what might be considered Christian values—kindness, empathy, caring and love—are important, but I haven't felt the need for religion in my life. I appreciate that religions create a community of people who support each other, though, which is especially important during tough times.

Have I tried alternative therapies? People I don't know have suggested all sorts of alternative approaches, including a ketogenic diet and meditation courses. Again, I'm sure they have value for some people, but they're not for me.

I'm sometimes asked what it's like reflecting on my life for this book. It's been surprisingly enjoyable. It's brought back some great memories that I hadn't thought about in years. Obviously, there's been pain at various times of my life, particularly during Mum's illness when I was a kid and all the challenges since my diagnosis. But I've appreciated reconnecting with people who I'd lost contact with, especially from my childhood, and meeting new people over the past year.

Mostly, though, the special moments of the last twelve months have centred around family—the time shared with Katie, the kids and close relatives. It's been special just being at home together, going out around Sydney or having short breaks away. As a partnership, Katie and I have raised three terrific children. We're proud of them. The kids should be proud of who they are, too. They're going to be wonderful citizens and wonderful people.

I've often said to them that they should work as hard as they can in their studies. But that's only one part of the contribution you can make to society. It's important to be kind and understanding, to be willing to work as part of a team and to be dedicated and committed. They're all elements in being a good human being.

One big change in my life in the past six months is that I've become a public figure. That's not something I've ever sought, but I've continued being really touched by the support from the wider community that has come with being better known. The hundreds of small moments of human connection—caring strangers wishing me all the best in the street, at work or as I've travelled around—have been genuinely uplifting.

I think people have connected so much with my story because I've been vulnerable and open about cancer. Unfortunately, the disease is so universal that many people identify with what I've been going through. Speaking at the Tour de Cure lunch in Brisbane in April, I found myself in tears during my speech, and I could see people in the audience were in tears as well. So many people came up to talk and take photos afterwards that Katie, Lucy and I didn't leave for another three hours.

More recently, when I was paying the bill after taking Katie out to dinner at a restaurant, a customer next to me at the counter congratulated me on being 'cured'. He was delighted. While that's not exactly medically accurate, I appreciated his heart and thoughtfulness.

I'm moved by these moments—even someone asking for a selfie when we're out—because it shows people have become at least a little invested in my treatment. The kids don't say anything when they're with me, but I wonder if it's valuable for them. It shows them how caring people can be and that they're hoping for the best for our family. Katie is more private but I know, deep down, that she's proud of what we're doing as a family to give hope to future glioblastoma patients.

Having said all that, I'd give up my higher public profile and all this support in a millisecond if I could have my non-cancerous life back.

Now that I've reached the point where I can imagine some sort of future, I've gone from feeling desperately unlucky to recognising how blessed I am in many ways. Cancer has made me value my life more. I've realised how finite it is. I've realised what's most important to me.

Cancer has also strengthened my belief in the importance of science. I've personally benefited from the scientific breakthroughs we've made in melanoma and the data we've generated. We've brought a brilliant team together and drawn on decades of knowledge and skill. There's an opportunity now for these breakthroughs to have an impact on another deadly cancer.

I've been asked at times how I feel about death. My answer is different now than it would have been even a month or two ago. It's hanging over me less heavily now, so I don't even want to think about it. A better question now might be: how do I feel about life?

I'd say I cherish it. We never know what's around the corner, so we should make the most of every moment we have.

When the end does come, how would I like people to remember me?

I'd like them to think of me as a decent person, who was kind of heart and who cared about his family and other people. I don't need them to think of me as courageous or inspirational—just someone who believed in science and, when faced with a terrible diagnosis, tried something bold and new.

I hope Katie and the kids know that I love them.

I hope I've contributed to medicine, pathology, research and melanoma management. I hope that when I'm gone, other brain tumour patients will live longer because of what we've tried.

I've loved my life. I hope they love theirs.

A NOTE FROM GARRY

Brainstorm has been an emotional project for me. In 2019, I was diagnosed out of the blue with Stage IV melanoma. A decade earlier, it would have been a death sentence. But the exceptional work of Melanoma Institute Australia meant immunotherapy gave me a shot at survival. Within months, medical oncologist Associate Professor Alex Menzies told me my scans showed the treatment was having a 'spectacular' effect on the cancer. Five years on, I'm effectively cured. Since then, Alex has told me that an article I wrote for *Good Weekend* magazine in *The Sydney Morning Herald* and *The Age*, later nominated for a Kennedy Award for the year's outstanding feature story, has been valuable for other melanoma patients going through immunotherapy treatment.

I didn't know Professor Richard Scolyer at the time, though we had both competed for Australia at the world triathlon championships in Chicago in 2015. Until my diagnosis, I was due to represent the country again at the 2019 world championships in Lausanne, where Richard and Professor Georgina Long, the co-medical directors of the Institute, both competed. After getting back to work at the *Herald*— and competing in triathlons again—I interviewed Richard a couple of times on the phone for stories about the Melanoma Institute's sun safety campaigns—then I read his troubling social media posts about being diagnosed with glioblastoma. Like hundreds of other people around the world, I was moved to send him messages of support.

Shortly after I wrote an opinion piece about why Richard and Georgina deserved their win as NSW Australians of the Year, he invited me for a coffee before work. I met him and Katie, his wife, at their home in Sydney's inner west, not far from mine. Richard said he had been approached by Allen & Unwin about telling his story and asked if I would like to write it. My immediate response was that I would be honoured to. It was a compelling story: a world-leading doctor risking an earlier death to trial a radical new type of brain cancer treatment. It had to be written quickly, though, because Richard might only have months left to live.

In the many hours we spent talking about his early life, his move into medicine and his melanoma work, my deep admiration never flagged for Richard as a brilliant and humble doctor who has devoted his life to helping other people.

Many times there were tears, especially at the thought that Richard would—barring a medical miracle—leave Katie without a husband and Emily, Matt and Lucy without a father. When we went for some bike rides, firstly while in Launceston for a family Christmas lunch then in Sydney, Richard was always great company. Despite what he was facing, he was remarkably optimistic.

As Richard became better known through two episodes of the ABC's *Australian Story* and winning 2024 Australian of the Year with Georgina, my aim with *Brainstorm* stayed the same. I thought it was important to do justice to his story while giving his kids a book that will remind them, if he is no longer around, who their father was.

Everyone who knows him, though, desperately hopes Richard will still be here for many years and that future glioblastoma patients will have a better chance of survival because of his courage, heart and humanity.

ACKNOWLEDGEMENTS

Brainstorm was written on Gadigal Land and I wish to acknowledge the Gadigal and Wangal peoples of the Eora nation as the traditional custodians of the land on which it was written.

There are many people who have contributed their time, patience and expertise to producing this book, and I would like to acknowledge and thank all of them for their help, assistance and guidance.

First and foremost, I would like to express a huge thank you to my collaborator, writer and now friend Garry Maddox for all his efforts in putting this book together. His hard work, dedication, flexibility and support are greatly appreciated. Tim Bauer, a true professional, took the wonderful cover photo. I am also grateful to the whole team at Allen & Unwin for their support and assistance, including Sally Heath, Courtney Lick, Bella Breden, Sarah Barrett, Sandra Buol and their colleagues.

I am filled with gratitude towards the medical teams who have contributed tirelessly to my medical care over the crazy journey since my glioblastoma came to light. I would particularly like to express my gratitude to my wife Katie and friends and colleagues, including Georgina Long, Brindha Shivalingam, Helen Rizos, Helen Wheeler, Michael Back, Alex Menzies, Maria Gonzales, Jamie Drummond, Artur Zembowicz and Margaret Zembowicz, for their key parts in my cancer journey. There are many, many other people who have supported me, and while there are too many to name individually, I am very grateful to each and every one of them.

I feel incredibly fortunate to have worked with amazing teams of people over the past 26 years at Royal Prince Alfred Hospital and Melanoma Institute Australia (MIA). Not only has it been very both rewarding and pleasurable working together but I consider many of our important contributions to the field have only been possible because of the ethos of teamwork at these organisations.

My pathology colleagues in the Tissue Pathology and Diagnostic Oncology Department at RPAH have been by my side through thick and thin and I am most appreciative of their support. I would especially like to thank Paul McKenzie, the late Stan McCarthy, Kerry Crotty and Peter Russell who, among others, inspired and supported me in the early stages of my pathology career at Royal Prince Alfred.

I am also extremely grateful to Kerry Crotty, Bill McCarthy, John Thompson, Stan McCarthy and others for the establishment of the inaugural MASCRI Pathology Fellowship. This position and my concurrent staff specialist appointment at Royal Prince Alfred led to me being mentored by John Thompson and Stan McCarthy, in particular, who soon became my very close friends. I can never thank them enough for their inspiration and guidance. Their support provided me with so many opportunities to contribute to the field, particularly in melanoma.

The team at MIA have also become my close friends and colleagues over decades and inspired me to work hard and try to make a difference. There are too many to thank individually but I am particularly grateful to John Thompson, Jon Stretch, Rick Kefford, Peter Hersey and Graham Mann early in my career. I cannot thank the brilliant multidisciplinary team of clinicians, researchers and support staff enough for all their hard work and support, particularly my co-medical director colleague Georgina Long, the 28 MIA senior clinicians and researchers who are MIA Faculty Members, MIA CEO Matthew Browne, Maria Gonzalez and Jennifer Durante, all MIA staff and the MIA Board. I also admire and appreciate the dedication of the brilliant MIA Translation Research Team based at the Charles Perkins Centre, the University of Sydney, including James Wilmott who commenced in 2008.

I am also incredibly appreciative of my amazing executive assistant, Kara Taylor. I am so grateful for her dedication and support, brilliant organisational abilities and management skills, as well as her friendship and kindness.

There are many national and international colleagues who have been incredibly supportive and helpful and become my good friends over the decades. Although there are too many to thank individually, I am especially indebted to Jeff Gershenwald, Klaus Busam, David Elder, Ray and Claire Barnhill, Artur Zembowicz, Daniela Massi, Michael Tetzlaff and the late Marty Mihm, among many others.

I feel extremely fortunate to have worked closely for years with my colleague and friend Georgina Long. I am very proud we have co-led our Institute and, as a team, achieved great outcomes for the melanoma field. Furthermore, I deeply appreciate her hard work and dedication to try to help me on my glioblastoma journey and make a difference to this field, too.

My friends and family have supported our family and me in everything; all of their contributions are greatly appreciated. I say thanks to my special friend Jim Finlay and his family for their friendship, generosity and support, as well as to my many close friends for their contributions to my numerous terrific experiences throughout my life. I am also particularly grateful to my relatives, including sisters-in-law Sally and Sophie, Mark's partner Anna, brothers-in-law Charlie and Lucian, and also to my many nieces and nephews, cousins, uncle and aunties and grandparents.

My loving parents Maurice and Jenny, thank you for believing in me from the very beginning and helping me to achieve my dreams. Your support and love through thick and thin have got me to where I am today.

My brother Mark, thank you for being such a good friend to me and a vital support to all our family, and for making so many sacrifices to support us. I am so grateful to have grown up with such a terrific role model.

To my wonderful children, Emily, Matthew and Lucy, thank you for your encouragement and good humour even on the most difficult days, and for putting a smile on my face every day. Katie and I are so proud of who each of you have become and I love you dearly.

Finally, to my amazing wife Katie, the best person I know, thank you for all you have done to support me through everything and for all you continue to do every single day. I feel so lucky to have you as my life partner. You are the most kind, caring and selfless person I have ever met, and fun to be around. I feel most fortunate to have you in my life and by my side, especially as we travel this difficult cancer journey together. That our paths crossed in such a timely manner and that we could share the rest of our lives is the favourite part of my existence. We have had some wonderful times together as a couple and as a family. I can never thank you enough for everything you have done and continue to do.

Richard

Warmest thanks to Heather and Kip for their unwavering love and support. And thanks also to my *Sydney Morning Herald* colleagues and friends, including editor Bevan Shields and national managing editor Monique Farmer.

Garry